The Time Is Now

40 Devotions to Empower You to Walk with Jesus in Any Season of Life

Katie Bergen

FIRST PRINT EDITION

LIBRARY AND ARCHIVES CANADA DATA
ISBN: 978-1-0689077-0-8

Publisher: Katie Bergen
Editor: Anna-Lisa Ptolemy
Cover Design & Formatting: WIESINGER Books

Dedication

To my husband Dennis: Thank you for encouraging and believing in me every step of the way. I know you kept saying that you are just an engineer and wouldn't be much help. But God still used all your giftings to make this a reality and I am grateful for your support.

Table of Contents

Introduction

I put my two-month-old down for a nap and prayed that he would sleep long enough that I could also get my two-year-old down for her nap half an hour later. When I finally shut my toddler's bedroom door, that feeling of freedom and exhilaration hit me. For at least the next few moments, I did not have anyone needing me. The dishwasher was clean and needed to be emptied and the laundry needed to be switched. My to-do list was beckoning to me. But I just did not have it in me anymore to do dishes and laundry, only to have more dishes and more laundry the next day and the next day and the day after that.

"I can't do it," I thought to myself. The anxiety of constantly being needed and worrying about everyone else felt like someone was sitting on top of me in a swimming pool and pushing me down until I was drowning. I couldn't get back up for a really deep breath of air. But as I closed the bedroom door, for a brief moment it felt like I could get back up to the surface for a quick breather if the kids slept long enough.

I was tired of feeling this way. I knew that all the times I was most connected with Jesus in my life were also the times that I felt the most peace. Peace that surpassed understanding. Peace even in the midst of busy exam schedules and practicums and work. No matter the circumstance, I always felt like I could breathe when I made it a priority to be close with God. Could it also bring me peace in the midst of dirty diapers and colicky babies? I knew that to be true in the past, and I was trusting that it would be true in my present.

So, I grabbed my iPad and I watched a sermon online. I did not actually start reading my Bible that day. I couldn't even do that, I was so tired. But I did what I could that day. And I laid on my couch watching the sermon series day after day during the small afternoon napping overlap time. I started taking notes. This turned into Bible reading.

Bible reading turned into praying. My afternoon Bible time during my kids' naps was like my moment to come up from under the water and breathe deeply.

Then one day I realized I wanted to get up before the kids because I couldn't wait until the middle of the day for that life-giving breath of air. I set my alarm and had the most peaceful moments with God before the day started to get out of control. It anchored me in the truth I needed to get through this time in my life.

And somehow the laundry and the dishes still always got done.

My kids are now much older as I write this. They are nine and seven. But what I have realized is that there will never be an easy time. One moment I am chasing after toddlers and the next moment I am driving kids to birthday parties and soccer practice. And, as my kids have grown, I have added new responsibilities. I expect this will continue. What I'm trying to say is we cannot wait for life to some day allow us the chance to spend time with Jesus. Because that time will never come unless we declare that we will not wait. Today is the perfect day to open up our Bible and our hearts for what God wants to do. There will never be a time when something won't seem more pressing than reading my Bible or spending my time in prayer. There will never be a time when I have more than 24 hours in a day. Life will always be complicated and full of excuses that seem valid. Those excuses will never be for anything better than what God can accomplish in my heart and in my life today when I open up my life to him.

The time is now.

So, I kept setting my alarm to wake me up before my children and I kept reading and praying. During naptime, I would pull out my Bible and prayer journal.

It is the power of God that keeps bringing me back into his Word again and again. Not my own power. If you are thinking I am different from you, I promise I am not.

God created us for relationship with him. In my mother's womb he created me with a need for him and to praise him: "I praise you because I am fearfully and wonderfully made; your works are wonderful, I know that full well" (Psalm 139:14, New International Version). He created us in a unique and beautiful way by which we would connect most intimately. The way we connect with God may look different for all of us. Some of us may connect deeply by writing songs and singing them, and some of us may find that connection with him in nature. Each season of life may look different too, but we are all created to have a relationship with God in our own ways. You were literally made to do this. And because you are holding this book in your hands, I believe you know that you were created for relationship with him and are looking for this connection in your life.

Maybe you've bought into the lie that you are able to do life all on your own. Let me ask you this: is it working? Or do you feel like you are missing out on the abundant life God has promised? You can have his peace in the middle of all of it. You can have his peace right now. You are made and fashioned by God for doing this. He created you for a relationship with him above all else. And the time is now to step into your God-given purpose.

This isn't about adding one more thing to your to-do list to make your head explode or guilt you for not spending time with Jesus. This is about prioritizing the best for your life, because Jesus promised us an abundant life and a lot of us are living on empty. It's about filling our tanks with the right fuel.

If I try to put water in my car's gas tank, it isn't going to run. If I fuel my life with the wrong things, it will not work as designed either.

This devotional is designed to help you develop a simple and easy routine to start every day and a variety of ideas, questions, and declarations to help you get into the habit of opening your Bible and giving time to God. This will start a beautiful journey with Jesus and leave you feeling full and not empty.

Jesus proclaims, "The thief comes only to steal and kill and destroy; I have come that they may have life, and have it to the full" (John 10:10, NIV).

I am not talking about just getting through the tough times. I am talking about thriving and having abundant life no matter what. Yes, even right now.

It's time to get started. Do not put it off for even one more day. You were meant to walk with God, today! He has so much waiting for you. One of my favourite passages in Proverbs says:

> Then he taught me, and he said to me, "Take hold of my words with all your heart; keep my commands, and you will live. Get wisdom, get understanding; do not forget my words or turn away from them. Do not forsake wisdom, and she will protect you; love her, and she will watch over you. The beginning of wisdom is this: Get wisdom. Though it cost all you have, get understanding. Cherish her, and she will exalt you; embrace her, and she will honor you. She will give you a garland to grace your head and present you with a glorious crown." Listen, my son, accept what I say, and the years of your life will be many. I instruct you in the way of wisdom and lead you along straight paths. When you walk, your steps will not be hampered; when you run, you will not stumble. Hold on to instruction, do not let it go; guard it well, for it is your life (4:4-13, NIV).

I don't know about you, but that sounds like exactly what I need for my life. I am excited to have you come along on this journey with me.

Each devotional will contain a few questions, a space to write out a prayer that you can read to God, and a declaration. Declarations are words of truth from scripture (like an affirmation) that we speak over our life.

I have also included an appendix (located on page 193) where you can find ideas on how to connect with Jesus and build a deep, meaningful, and life-changing relationship. There is no minimum time commitment or correct amount of Bible reading or prayer. This is all between you and God. I am just here to give you encouragement and help you get started. This book is not meant to pressure you, but to empower you to step into the most rewarding journey of bringing Jesus close to you in any season of your life.

A Word on Declarations

Many of you may not have encountered the idea of speaking Bible declarations before. Neither had I until a few years ago. I joined a small group where the leader would speak scripture and we would all repeat it after her. This group was on Zoom during COVID, which made speaking declarations out loud feel even more awkward to try.

She began by saying the first declaration.

"The one who is in you is greater than the one who is in the world" (1 John 4:4, NIV).

And then I opened my mouth and 15 or so other women and I began to speak those words together.

"The one who is in you is greater than the one who is in the world."

WOW! It gave me chills. Hearing women speak the word of God together was extremely powerful.

We continued on.

"Be strong in the Lord and in his mighty power" (Ephesians 6:10, NIV).

"I will say of the Lord, 'He is my refuge and my fortress, my God, in whom I trust'" (Psalm 91:2, NIV).

The enemy cannot read our minds. He sees that we open our Bibles. But it is when we speak the truth of God that he can hear the strength of God within us. You can feel your whole body begin to relax when you declare the truth of God out loud. Your enemy flees.

I encourage you to speak each of the following declarations out loud, boldly and with the authority of Christ. It might feel awkward. But you will unleash the power of God that immediately disarms the enemy.

You are picking up a sword of strength from God. Declaring God's truth out loud will empower you, encourage you, and give you life.

"Come near to God and he will come near to you" (James 4:8, NIV).

Get ready to live as you were created!

Day 1: Giving out of Poverty

I sat in my Wednesday morning Bible study with my five-month-old baby on my lap. She was restless. I tried to put her down on the floor, but she fussed. I tried to rock her to sleep, but there were too many distractions. I was worried she was bothering everyone. I was sweating. I was barely able to concentrate, making my attempt to be there feel utterly worthless. I couldn't socialize, I couldn't focus. All I was getting out of it was frustration.

I finally mustered up all my courage and walked my daughter over to the childcare area and tried to drop her off.

Big fat fail.

She cried. I couldn't stomach the anxiety of trying anymore. Dropping her off was not an option.

The last five months had already been a hard-hitting reality that motherhood was all-encompassing. Now, I was not even able to continue on with the book study.

I was trying to do something that was good: a Christian small group book study to learn about God and make Christian friends and have that support during this time. I was after something GOOD. God would make a way.

I prayed that the separation anxiety would go away. It didn't.

I actually became really mad at God. This was something positive I was attempting to do with my time. The Bible tells us to meet together and to study God's word (Hebrews 10:25). God was not rewarding me for my effort or heart's desire by answering that prayer. He did not make a way for me to be there. I didn't understand how this was not part of his plan for me. Wouldn't a Bible study align with (what I assumed was) his will for me? He never did make a way for me to be part of that Bible study.

I finally prayed one last prayer. I told God that I was willing. I would show up in the small way I could by reading the book alone, even if he wouldn't grant my request to participate in the Bible study group in person. I would do the study even if he would not remove the obstacles to my being there. I reasoned that one day I could at least face God and announce, "I did everything I could to be there", and ask him, "Why didn't you answer my prayer?"

Every semester, instead of signing up for a group, I browsed through the book study options, bought the book, and did it on my own. No group. No leaving my house. Just my book and I during the occasional naptime. For the next four years I did not attend a Bible study group with my children.

I'm sure there are parts of my story that resonate with you. Reasons it feels impossible to pray, read the Bible, attend church, join the small group, lead the small group, volunteer on a Sunday, or whatever it is for you.

You're too tired for Bible study this week/season/semester.

You're too tired to wake up early and read your Bible and pray.

You're too tired to stay up and read your Bible and pray.

You feel excluded, so why should you go and include others?

This season is really tough, so maybe other people should serve me!

And finally, how can I do that with my kids?

There is an account of a poor widow in the Bible who also didn't have a lot to give.

Mark 12:41-44 (NIV) says,

> Jesus sat down opposite the place where the offerings were put and watched the crowd putting their money into the temple treasury. Many rich people threw in large amounts. But a poor widow came and put in two very small copper coins, worth only a few cents. Calling his disciples to him, Jesus said, "Truly I tell you, this poor widow has put more into the

> treasury than all the others. They all gave out of their wealth; but she, out of her poverty, put in everything—all she had to live on.

Jesus did not praise the people who gave out of their wealth, but those who gave out of their poverty.

But what if he didn't just mean money?

What if when we do not feel loved, we give what love we have?

What if when we don't have more than a few minutes, we give them to God?

What if when we don't feel like we belong, we invite others into belonging?

I think Jesus is pleased when we give out of the poverty in our lives instead of out of our wealth. We give him what little time we have. We love the few people around us we can. We serve with the abilities we've been given, no matter how small or insignificant we think they are. When we put in all we have, God will do the rest.

A dear friend once said to me, "not being able to do everything isn't an excuse not to do anything."

I gave God what I had in that season. I read a few books at home during naptime. He met me alone in my house with my book studies. He taught me the value of alone time with him. And when my life switched from one child to two and I walked into a season of postpartum anxiety, I knew that alone time with God would always be available to me in any season of life. This season taught me perseverance in chasing after God. He taught me that although community and attending church and being able to focus fully while there are good things, they might not be possible in every season. We can give God what we have where we are at, right now. I was forced to spend that time alone with God, but it taught me the value of being in his presence first and foremost. This book was born out of that time. It forced me to see that offering God exactly what I did have was all that was needed.

Declaration

Now to him who is able to do immeasurably more than all we ask or imagine, according to his power that is at work within us (Ephesians 3:20, NIV).

Questions

In this season, what are you lacking that you would like to give to God? (e.g., time/money/patience)

What are you currently contributing to God's kingdom?

Do you feel called to do more to grow your relationship with God? What do you feel called to start doing to build a closer relationship with Jesus?

Prayer

Write a prayer to God asking him to help you determine what you need to start doing to build a closer relationship with him. If you already know what you need to start doing, then write a prayer asking God to help you commit to the steps you need to take to make that happen.

Sample: Father, help me know what spiritual disciplines I need to begin and what I need to surrender to grow closer to you. In this season of my life and with exactly what I have to give to you right now, I need you show me how we can have a closer relationship. Please help me to trust that you will grow my faith in you and that time with you will change me more than I can ask or imagine.

Day 2: The Cost of Following Jesus

It was time to take my son to his soccer practice, so I went into the living room to tell him to turn off his video game and get ready.

"Just let me finish this level first!"

I really can't stand it when my kids make excuses when it's time to go.

"We have to be at soccer in 20 minutes, so you need to get your stuff on now!"

Just like a mom reminds her son about what his priorities are (soccer over video games), Jesus reminds us that the time is now for us to get to work for his kingdom. In Matthew 9:37 Jesus said to his disciples, "The harvest is plentiful but the workers are few" (NIV).

Like my invitation to my son to get moving, Jesus invites us to join him in becoming fishers of men. But just like my son, we often make excuses. We will start the group, join the group, open the Bible, or read the book when life slows down or when this or that finishes up.

In Luke 9:57-62, Jesus meets three men and has three similar encounters. I'm using The Message version here because I find the dialogue comparable to how these same conversations would have played out today.

> On the road someone asked if he could go along. "I'll go with you, wherever," he said. Jesus was curt: "Are you ready to rough it? We're not staying in the best inns, you know." Jesus said to another, "Follow me." He said, "Certainly, but first excuse me for a couple of days, please. I have to make arrangements for my father's funeral." Jesus refused. "First things first. Your business is life, not death. And life is urgent:

> Announce God's kingdom!" Then another said, "I'm ready to follow you, Master, but first excuse me while I get things straightened out at home." Jesus said, "No procrastination. No backward looks. You can't put God's kingdom off till tomorrow. Seize the day."

Jesus is saying the time is now. Our excuses do not cut it with him. He created us to live a relationship with him even in the midst of busy schedules, dirty diapers, carpools, exams, and deadlines. He also created us to need a close relationship in the middle of the much harder things in life, such as losing a job, dealing with illness, and burying a loved one. We are all doing wonderful things with our lives. I don't believe Jesus is asking us to quit our jobs to read the Bible all day, but he is telling us that God's kingdom is right now. There is an urgency in Jesus' words.

When things are overwhelming and busy, we need more Jesus, not less. More of his patience, more of his love, more of God's grace and supply and less of the world and the empty promises that leave us drained.

I wonder if we hear a bit of ourselves when we think of the excuses the men gave Jesus. Jesus is saying, "follow me," and these are our excuses:

"But first, let me raise my children."

"But first, let me get this next promotion at work."

"But first, let me accomplish these goals."

"But first, let me do the laundry/dishes/vacuuming."

"But first, let me enjoy the comforts that I have worked very hard for."

"But first, let me scroll through my social media feeds."

We cannot put God's kingdom off until tomorrow. The invitation is for today.

My son's soccer practice starts at 5:30pm. He cannot be part of a soccer team and just show up when he feels like he has played enough video games for the day. Would there ever be enough video games?

There is always another level, a new world, a new game to try. He will never play enough video games.

We are the same as my son. There will always be more to keep us engaged in something other than Jesus. There will always be a "just one more level" excuse. A walk with Jesus day in and day out is much more like choosing a healthy game of soccer with friends over solo video game time, don't you think?

The time is now.

Seize the day. Don't look back. As Jesus said, "Your business is life not death."

Declaration

But as for me and my household, we will serve the Lord (Joshua 24:15b, NIV).

Questions

Finish the sentence, as many times as you want:

But first let me…

Do you feel like you have missed out on an invitation Jesus extended to you in the past? What was your excuse? How did you feel about missing out?

Prayer

Write a prayer asking Jesus to show you the next steps you can take to prioritize the kingdom of God. If there are things you are clinging to that you should let go of, ask him to help you release them.

Day 3:
Half-Truths

We don't like to talk about Satan. It is uncomfortable, and I feel this dark heaviness even typing his name. But if we are going to have victory in our lives through Christ, we must acknowledge him. He is a very real enemy who does not want me or you to ever open our Bibles. He doesn't want the Word of God to saturate our souls. The enemy wants nothing more than for you to stay away from reading God's Word because he knows how absolutely powerful it is when you spend time in the Bible. He is going to put up a fight to keep you out of the Word. If you think that it is going to be easy to get into a new habit of reading your Bible every day, think again.

I am here to tell you that the enemy of your soul is waging an all-out attack on your life. But Satan doesn't need to bring you down all the way to still bring you down. He is happy to let you believe you are getting enough Jesus in your life, even when there is so much more available to you. Let me explain. I think a lot of Christians can settle for a little bit of God, like church on Sunday and maybe the odd small group or volunteer role. He is okay with letting you think you are getting the fullness of Christ and abundant life this way.

Do you ever feel like when you want to read the Bible, a million other more amusing and important-feeling distractions begin to come up? Scrolling your phone or that pile of dishes both seem so much more alluring than a few minutes in God's Word, somehow. What a sneaky serpent he must be if he can make that pile of dishes look so enticing.

To fight back on this (which you will need to do), you need to know your opponent and the weapons that he is choosing to use against you. This way you can equip yourself with the right defensive weapons. There is a saying that goes, "don't bring a knife to a gunfight".

When I listen to women talk about their busyness and their inability to spend time in God's Word, I notice a few common ways the enemy has won this battle in their lives.

The enemy loves to use half-truths as a weapon against us because a half-truth will have some validity. One way the enemy does this is by quoting scripture.

In Matthew 4:6, the enemy actually throws scripture at Jesus while he is being tempted in the desert to try and cause him to sin. "'If you are the Son of God,' he said, 'throw yourself down. For it is written: He will command his angels concerning you, and they will lift you up in their hands, so that you will not strike your foot against a stone'" (Matthew 4:6, NIV).

But in verse 7, Jesus responds by quoting scripture back at him:

"Jesus answered him, 'It is also written: Do not put the Lord your God to the test.'"

Jesus knew the Word of God. Therefore, he knew when the Word was being twisted. The devil was throwing Him a "half-truth" and he recognized it.

I have heard women say, "God knows I am busy and he will meet me where I am at" as an example of a half-truth. Typical scriptures we use to defend this idea are when Jesus met the woman at the well or when Jesus saved the prostitute from her accusers about to stone her. While these are true accounts of Jesus' ministry, the point of these stories is not Jesus saying, "you do not need to come to me."

In fact, James 4:8a declares, "Draw near to God, and he will draw near to you" (English Standard Version).

Jesus told the woman about to be stoned to go and leave her life of sin (John 8:11). The woman at the well got up and ran back into town to tell people about her encounter with Jesus (John 4:28). Jesus met these women where they were, but they didn't stay where Jesus found them. They took action.

Another substantial half-truth the enemy uses is a variation of the original sin recorded in the third chapter of Genesis, when the serpent is tempting Eve.

The serpent wants Eve to feel like God is holding something back from her.

"You will not certainly die," the serpent said to the woman. "For God knows that when you eat from it your eyes will be opened, and you will be like God, knowing good and evil." (Genesis 3:4-5, NIV).

The enemy is speaking to us today and telling us that if we spend time in God's Word and set aside time to be in relationship with him that we will not have time to accomplish everything else we need to get done. He is lying and telling us that we are missing out on something important to us if we spend time with God.

Do you hear that hissing sound and the serpent whispering these lies to you, slightly dressed up with a bit of truth?

"Did God really say that you need to spend time with him?"

"God doesn't expect you to make space in this season of life for him. The women of the Bible never did."

"The people who spend time with God daily are different than you. They don't have [insert your excuse here] to deal with like you do."

"You have too much to do, and you will not get everything done if you take time to be with God every day."

Remarkably, I have never encountered a single person saying anything even close to the following statements:

"I spent time in God's Word today. What a waste. I got nothing else accomplished."

"I read my Bible this morning, and everything else in my day got messed up because of it."

I often hear excuses with half-truths. But what I don't often hear is women declaring full truths. Full truths such as, "Jesus is holding me together today," or "I am loved and I am enough because Jesus is walking closely with me." We only see these full truths in our lives when we give our time and energy to Jesus and discover that nothing is ever held back from us.

So, what do we need to bring to the fight if the weapons against us are half-truths? The weapons you fight back with successfully are full truths. Knowing the Word of God. Carrying the Word of God with you in your heart. Maybe you do not have it perfectly memorized word for word, but you know it, and you know the one who wrote it. It cannot then be twisted and used against you to steal the peace and love Jesus is offering you in this season of life.

It does take time and energy to build up an arsenal of truth. This book won't give you the easy way forward. I am telling you the opposite! It won't be easy, but the victory is yours when you fight with the weapons that will actually beat your enemy.

Declaration

From the ends of the earth, I cry to you for help when my heart is overwhelmed. Lead me to the towering rock of safety, for you are my safe refuge, a fortress where my enemies cannot reach me (Psalm 61:2-3, New Living Translation).

Questions

What are your top justifications for skipping devotional time?

What do you think Jesus wants to accomplish in your heart during devotional time? Why do you think the enemy wants to take that away from you?

Prayer

Thank you, Jesus, for wanting to do life together with me. For pursuing my heart even when my days are overwhelming. I trust that you will make a way through the busyness. I trust that your truth is full truth. Help me to follow you even when distractions and excuses pile up.

Day 4:
Put on Your Oxygen Mask First

I don't know about you, but any time I fly anywhere, by the time we get to our seats and the attendants begin the safety instructions I am so tired that I just tune them out. I've heard them so many times before. It's nothing new. I have the whole script memorized. This is how you use a seatbelt. Put on my own mask before assisting other people. Got it.

I personally do not know anyone who has ever been in an airplane that lost its cabin pressure, but I am sure if you were to ask any mom what they would do in that situation if they were flying with their children, they would say that they would put an oxygen mask on their children before they put one on themselves.

As loving as that is, it could actually be a very deadly mistake.

In the event of a loss of cabin pressure you have very little time before you will develop symptoms of hypoxia which includes lack of coordination and judgement, rendering it extremely difficult to then put your own mask on. This is why they instruct you to put your own mask on first, because you might not have time to put on someone else's before your own (Chodosh, 2018).

When it comes to our survival and the survival of our loved ones, we must put our own mask on first before assisting others. And you know where this is going: this concept isn't limited to an airplane cabin.

We often put our children's needs ahead of our own, which is exactly what our motherly instincts tell us to do because caring for our children is of the utmost importance. We see a long to-do list and make a decision to check off those boxes. There are a lot of things in our day that we are required to get done. We need to feed our children. We need to go to work. However, we do not pursue our spiritual health with the same survival need as the other boxes we check off during our day. We make the choice to focus only on those things and not on our walk with Jesus. But is it possible that a close walk with Jesus will make us better mothers? Better employees? Better friends? Better spouses? When we take care of ourselves spiritually first, it will allow us to assist everyone else around us.

Creating that space and investing time in a relationship with Jesus might not be the first box you check off at the beginning of your day. The demands of a hungry toddler do not go away when we open our Bible. But those demanding time and attention from us can only take control if we let them. We need to take care of our spiritual well-being before everything else because it is going to be the oxygen we need to survive and to assist everyone else. Sacrificing our spiritual health is bad for us and it's bad for everyone around us, too.

When we spend our days securing everyone else's masks, we might not end up with deadly low oxygen saturation levels. But we will reach dangerously low levels of patience, love, endurance, grace, and closeness with Jesus. We might not face imminent physical death. But we quickly find ourselves spiritually dead.

Proverbs 4:20-22 beautifully illustrates a life where we are receiving that sufficient life-giving Word of God: "My child, pay attention to what I say. Listen carefully to my words. Don't lose sight of them. Let them penetrate deep into your heart, they bring life to those who find them and healing to their whole body" (NLT).

The Word of God is life to our spirit just as oxygen is life to our physical bodies.

We spend our days trying to survive on the leftovers. The Netflix show you watch after you crash at the end of the day is not meant to be life-giving or spirit-filling. But we run to that. Believe me when I tell you that it isn't enough to give you the life abundant that you are craving in your heart. What is needed for survival cannot be swapped out for imitation. The amount of oxygen in a depressurized airplane is not adequate for survival, even if we can breathe it in. In the same way, nothing else we reach for will sustain us spiritually the way the Word of God will.

In addition, if oxygen levels drop slowly, it can be difficult to detect the hypoxia that comes on gradually. Pilots in training will go into a hypobaric chamber to experience hypoxia in themselves and in others so they can recognize it (Chodosh, 2018). Would you recognize it in yourself if the saturation of God in your life dropped to dangerously low levels?

"He humbled you, causing you to hunger and then feeding you with manna, which neither you nor your ancestors had known, to teach you that man does not live on bread alone but on every word that comes from the mouth of the Lord" (Deuteronomy 8:3, NIV).

This is hard. It goes against your instinct. Our instinct to put the mask on someone else first is wrong.

A lot of us are walking along as if we are gasping for precious air. Jesus offers us so much life-sustaining power. Just as he created us to need oxygen, he created us to need him. We do not need to suffer in a state of spiritual hypoxia.

Like the instructions from the flight attendant in case of an emergency:

"Put on your mask and breathe normally."

He has the power to bring life to your dry bones.

> Then he said to me, "Prophesy to these bones and say to them, 'Dry bones, hear the word of the Lord! This is what the Sovereign Lord says to these bones: I will make breath enter you, and you will come to life. I will attach tendons to you and make flesh come upon you and cover you with skin; I will put breath in you, and you will come to life. Then you will know that I am the Lord'" (Ezekiel 37:4-6, NIV).

Declaration

You will keep in perfect peace those whose minds are steadfast, because they trust in you (Isaiah 26:3, NIV).

Questions

What is on your to-do list before spending time with God? List as many things as you can that you place as a priority.

Which of the above things could you move until after you have spent a few moments with God? (e.g., those which are not time sensitive priorities or things can be left for another day)? Circle them.

Write out a plan for how you can re-do your routine to put time for God before other lesser things. Make a swap with some of your daily routines, such as what you do when you first wake up in the morning or right before your lunch break at work. Write this plan down here.

Prayer

God, I pray that you would make known to me what it is that you want me to give up or put lower on my list of priorities for you. Show me which distractions are not life-giving but rather life-taking. Please help me to put what matters first and be excited to spend time with you and your Word.

Day 5: Driving In Darkness

When I was in my early twenties, I had an old car with an after-market CD player. The day I got that stereo was a thrilling moment! No longer would I have to make tapes or scan the radio to find something enjoyable to listen to.

It didn't last long. One morning I found my car had been broken into and my beloved CD player was gone. Now I had no radio AND no CDs. Having an old mix tape seemed like a dream now.

I eventually did buy another CD player. I thought at the time that the thief decided to do me a huge favour. They didn't cut any wires, just nicely unplugged it. I figured the bright side of all this was that I wouldn't need to pay another installation fee. I could do it myself.

I easily plugged the stereo into the wires hanging out of my dash. Then I shoved the CD player in. It was a tight fit. I had to really jam it all the way in, but my economical installation seemed to work. It almost felt too good to be true. And eventually, I would realize that it was.

On my first late night drive I realized my dashboard didn't light up anymore. I couldn't see how fast I was going in the dark. This wasn't a problem in the daytime, and at night I would just drive to keep up with the traffic around me. A slight inconvenience, really. I drove around enjoying my tunes and feeling pleased with myself for being able to roll with the punches so well.

Then a day came when I was driving home from a friend's house out in the country after dark. I had to drive through a construction zone. I was all alone on the highway and didn't have anyone to match speed with. I was flying blind, so to speak. But nevertheless, I made it home, and filed that incident away as "a one-time thing".

However, a few months later all of this caught up with me when for the first time in my life I could hear a siren behind me and I saw the dreaded red and blue lights in my rear-view mirror. I pulled over, a little unsure about what this was about. I hadn't done anything illegal that I could think of. But then the police officer asked me if I knew my taillights were out. I had been driving around with zero lights on the back of my car. YIKES! My installation had apparently triggered an electrical problem on the outside of my car. That thought terrified me. I had been out on that highway all alone in the dark a few weeks earlier, completely unlit. I told the police officer that I didn't know about the taillights. He let me off with a warning.

I have no idea what actually happened with my electrical system in my car when I installed my own stereo, but here's what I do know.

We can drive around in the dark without our gauges showing us the information we need to drive safely. We can probably do this for a while before it catches up to us. We can guess that we are going the right speed or that we have enough fuel for our journey. I ignored the electrical problem inside my car, but what I didn't know was that there were no lights on the outside of my car either. It was covered in darkness too.

And really, the inside of my car wasn't illuminated, so it makes sense that the outside wasn't illuminated either. I should have known.

When there was no light inside my car on my gauges, there was no light for anyone outside my car to follow me safely.

I thought I could see well enough by using the streetlights while I was driving. But that wasn't enough. It wasn't inside my vehicle. I had to have real light inside my car to drive around safely.

If we do not invest in the spiritual light within us, we will not display any light outside ourselves either. In Luke 11:35-36, Jesus gives us a stern warning regarding our internal light: "Make sure that the light you think you have is not actually darkness. If you are filled with light, with no dark corners, then your whole life will be radiant, as though a floodlight were filling you with light" (NLT).

God's Word is like lighting up the dash inside the car. When God's Word is in us, we can navigate where we are going. And we also have light on the outside of us that can light other people's path on their journey to Jesus. Our instruments are working properly. We are safe for the journey. It is not enough to just get by on the light around us. Jesus wants his light inside of us.

Declaration

The Lord is my light and my salvation—whom shall I fear? The Lord is the stronghold of my life— of whom shall I be afraid? (Psalm 27:1, NIV).

Questions

When you do not have a close relationship with God, what are some of the ways that your light becomes dim on the outside? Do you find yourself in a particular type of mood? Do you withdraw from activities? Are there sins that you begin to engage in? What are the tell-tale signs that you need to fix your internal dashboard lighting?

When you have a close relationship with Jesus, what are some of the ways that your light is bright? Do you engage with people in your life differently? Handle things differently? Feel differently about yourself?

Prayer

Set a timer for one minute. Sit and just listen to God. Write down what he is saying to you.

Day 6:
Hangry Lions and Busy Schedules

It starts with my child asking me for a snack a little too close to dinner. I tell them dinner is coming and they have to wait, but as the waiting goes on, they get increasingly cranky and in my face. They whine more, bother their siblings, and become increasingly angry until finally dinner is served. If you've been around a really hungry kid longer than a few minutes, you are probably familiar with the mood called "hangry": hungry and angry.

1 Peter 5:8 (NIV) says, "Be alert and of sober mind. Your enemy the devil prowls around like a roaring lion looking for someone to devour."

The devil is hangry and he wants to devour you. He is going to be increasingly annoying and in your face until he gets you to move further away from Jesus.

So, when the demands of life (which are not bad things in and of themselves) such as motherhood, jobs, school, extracurricular activities, family events, birthday parties, etc. start to pile up, we push away the time that we spend in the Word of God to make room. We can begin to feel that because this season of life is busy, our need for scripture to infiltrate our hearts daily can take a back seat. Jesus understands our schedules are busy (or so we reason), so it will be ok if we do not spend time reading the Word of God right now.

However, the devil does not stop prowling around just because your schedule gets filled up. He does not stop trying to destroy you because you have little kids right now, or because you have a big project at work or an endless to-do list. My kids do not stop asking for food because I am busy with something else.

Our lives may not turn directly to sin and fall completely apart if we ignore our spiritual life in this way. We can hold it together pretty well even at the busiest of times. However, the enemy doesn't need to actually destroy you to win. He just wants you to neglect a full life with Jesus. He just wants to distract you. He wants to disarm you. He wants to minimize the impact you have for Jesus. That really is enough for his purposes. These little compromises pull us away from Jesus and erode any possibility of a deep relationship with him.

When my kids were little, the other little kid moms around me all talked about how they didn't have time for Bible reading. "It's okay, it's just a season." They would all encourage each other that this season would pass. But as my kids have gotten older, my schedule has actually gotten busier! One busy season bleeds into another until that is all that we have ever had: busy schedules and weary hearts disconnected from Jesus.

That is what the devil wants. We are so eager to complacently accept that we are a generation of women, moms, and boss ladies who are too tired for Bible reading and time with Jesus. We can easily believe the lie that we can set aside devotional time and a deep intimate relationship with Jesus for another time. We believe the lie that a better time will come later. I promise you, it won't.

Instead, we can boldly decide that being a distracted and disarmed group of women isn't what we are going to accept for ourselves. We can hold our homes and families together by using the power of God to equip us for how demanding each season will be. We do not have to believe the lie that adding Jesus would be the straw that breaks the camel's back and causes all that we are trying to build with our lives to fall apart due to a now overpacked schedule.

We will raise our children with the powerful words of God equipping them, because the powerful Word of God is equipping us. We will lead with confidence in whatever we set out to accomplish because we are empowered by the Creator of the Universe. There is so much strength in declaring that we will not be taken down by our enemy, at any time, because we have a God that has already declared victory over our lives.

There is no season that we don't need Jesus!

In my life I see it play out daily. Satan is busy trying to distract me from my mission to raise my family and teach my kids to love Jesus. But I will not buy into the lie that I do not need a close and intimate relationship with Jesus in my parenting season.

We do not have to be tired, weary, and vulnerable to this hangry lion.

John 10:10 (NIV) says, "The thief comes only to steal and kill and destroy. I came that they may have life and have it abundantly."

Jesus doesn't want us to feel drained by his Word. The exact opposite is true. It's the thief that is stealing and killing and destroying us. Not the Word of God. This Word is giving us life and life abundantly. In every season.

And so, I turn up the worship music and joyfully prepare dinner for my hangry children as they whine away, letting the rhythm of the song saturate my soul and allowing Christ's power to move in me. Even in the busy phase of hangry kids.

Declaration

For I can do everything through Christ, who gives me strength (Philippians 4:13, New Living Translation).

Questions

What are the reasons that you want to have Jesus in your life even when it can be hard to make time?

What excuses do you make to justify putting Jesus last?

Do you ever compare yourself to other women who regularly spend time with Jesus? How do your comparisons make you feel?

Prayer

Write a prayer to God asking him to empower you to rise up and put Jesus in His rightful place in your life.

Day 7: Time Tithing

Over the years I have spent a lot of time putting my best foot forward. I have planned outfits for family photoshoots that were coordinated for perfection and took days of energy and many trips to the store. I have sifted through 30 photos to pick the best one for posting on social media. I know how to showcase the best parts of me for the world to see. It takes a lot of energy to maintain a perfect image.

But do we ever offer ourselves up to God in the same way and try to give him the best of ourselves? Do we give him our leftovers or do we honour him with the best of who we are?

Proverbs 3:9 commands, "Honor the Lord with your wealth and with the best part of everything you produce" (NIV).

Tithing our money is typically seen as giving God 10% of our earnings. More specifically, giving God the first 10% of first fruits. In Leviticus 27:30 we read, "A tithe of everything from the land, whether grain from the soil or fruit from the trees, belongs to the Lord; it is holy to the Lord" (NIV).

We are giving back to God what was his to begin with. And make no mistake, time is a precious commodity to us all, much like money. It is the ultimate non-renewable resource on Earth. Our time here is finite and it belongs to God. Every day is a gift from him.

Yet, we spend most of our time putting our best 10% out into the world to impress others who do not truly decide our value instead of giving our best 10% to God, who already has claimed our value.

We should view tithing our time the way we view tithing our money.

We can give the best of our time to God. We can give him the best of who we are. We can prioritize to give him the time when we are most awake and alert. The time we could otherwise devote to pursuing things that are meaningless. We can devote our gifts and talents that he has given us to serving in his kingdom too.

It's not wrong to spend time doing other things that aren't exclusively for the kingdom of God. But there is always more power in everything we do when we put the best of ourselves into spending time with God instead of just the leftovers at the end of the day.

This is not an act of pouring into a black hole where every effort directed towards God is lost in space.

We can trust that God will still make a way for us to accomplish everything we need to do during our day even if we set aside time for him. In the same way he challenges us to trust that giving him the first 10% of our earnings will bless us to overflowing, could we trust that giving him the first fruits of our time he can also bless us to overflowing? I believe we absolutely can trust that God is not holding anything back from us when we choose to spend time in close relationship with him.

"'Bring the whole tithe into the storehouse, that there may be food in my house. Test me in this,' says the Lord Almighty, 'and see if I will not throw open the floodgates of heaven and pour out so much blessing that there will not be room enough to store it'" (Malachi 3:10, NIV).

Giving the world our best only gives diminishing returns. It doesn't satisfy. "I have seen all the things that are done under the sun; all of them are meaningless, a chasing after the wind" (Ecclesiastes 1:14, NIV). It leaves us worn out, broke, and feeling empty. Any good feels are just temporary. We are still looking for more. You've tried it, so you know it doesn't provide lasting significance. It doesn't work for what you buy, and it won't work for how you spend your time either.

Jesus is beckoning us to start with him, not just finish with him. It won't matter what we have left for the world after we allow him to infiltrate our hearts and fill us to overflowing. The longer you seek him first, the more you realize that lasting fullness and meaning come from Jesus and Jesus alone.

Declaration

But seek first his kingdom and his righteousness, and all these things will be given to you as well (Matthew 6:33, NIV).

Questions

What do you give the first 10% of your time to each day?

What do you try to accomplish with your best energy each day?

What do you give your energy and time to that you do not feel God would be pleased about?

If you were to give up to 10% of your time to God each day, what would you like God to accomplish in your heart and life?

Prayer

Write a prayer asking God to show you how you can release the specific things that are holding you back from surrendering your time to God.

Day 8:
The Power of Jesus

In the HBO series Chernobyl (based on the nuclear reactor disaster in Ukraine in 1986), there is a scene shortly after the nuclear reactor explodes where a firefighter responding to the accident curiously picks up a piece of radioactive graphite. This graphite was from the tip of the nuclear control rods from inside the reactor. Graphite just looks like a chunk of carbon. Pencils are made from graphite. There is nothing visibly exciting or scary about this piece of graphite. After inspecting it for a moment, he tosses it down to get on with fighting the fire. Shortly after, we see the firefighter sitting on the ground, his hand bloody as he screams in agony.

This man couldn't see the powerful ferociousness of the radioactivity within this piece of graphite. The power it held was invisible. Radiation cannot be seen. But the power of it can be felt. The force of its power was not reflected in its appearance. Spending time in God's Word is a bit like that. It can seem boring and monotonous. It may look like a plain old chunk of graphite and not like a piece of shimmering gold.

The radioactive graphite did not appear to hold a force whose power is so strong that the energy it creates and leaves in its wake cannot be undone. In the same way, the power of God's Word in your life will be a force so strong that it has the power to fight spiritual forces of darkness, turning them into light "and the darkness can never extinguish it" (John 1:5b, NLT).

God's Word has the power to separate light from darkness. Truth from lies. Love from hate. Freedom from bondage. And once these things happen, they cannot be undone.

You must know the power you hold when you pick up the Bible. But unlike the radioactive graphite's deadly power, the hidden power of the Word of God will give you abundant life.

When I first began my journey with daily Bible reading, I was just trying to have enough Jesus to sustain myself for the day or week. I really did not know the power that I was holding and the potential it would have to change my life or my heart.

It challenged so many thoughts and beliefs that I carried that I realized did not reflect truth. I was forced to change what I believed and it challenged me to surrender what I think or even what I was raised to think about what Jesus says.

It gave me strength and courage to conquer areas of my life that I was in bondage to and to conquer the lies of the enemy.

It gave me perseverance to keep running this race in a world where everything else is demanding my attention or trying to tear me down piece by piece.

You will have to grab your Bible and pick it up when you don't feel like it. You will have to read the words when you are not feeling them every day. You will wonder, "is this even working?" But truly there is nothing you could hold that is more valuable or soul changing.

When it comes to radiation, there can be a huge dose all at once, such as the one at the nuclear reactor in Chernobyl. But even a lower amount can still cause destruction to your body. In fact, even a very low dose can increase your chances of developing cancer (WHO, 2023).

We can see parallels between small doses of radiation and the power of God. Any small daily commitments have tremendous power to transform your heart, even very small daily doses of truth being tucked inside your heart. Instead of damaging your DNA like radiation does (Canadian Nuclear Safety Commission, 2019), the Word of God has the power to change the DNA of your heart to create a new you.

Proverbs 3:13-18 offers us a glimpse of this promise:

> Blessed is the one who finds wisdom, and the one who gets understanding, for the gain from her is better than gain from silver and her profit better than gold. She is more precious than jewels, and nothing you desire can compare with her.

> Long life is in her right hand; in her left hand are riches and honor. Her ways are ways of pleasantness, and all her paths are peace. She is a tree of life to those who lay hold of her; those who hold her fast are called blessed (NIV).

When we spend our days trying to achieve these things without the power of the Word of God, we end up exhausted. But the Bible promises us everything and more. Its power is undeniable.

If you think radiation is powerful, how much mightier is the one who created its force? Who thought up uranium and plutonium and then created them? And he can give you strength that has no half-life and doesn't decay when you tuck its truth in your heart. Its force is eternal. The light you carry with the Word of God inside of you is like taking the most powerful thing in all existence with you wherever you go. The energy that comes from the truth of the Word of God and his power in your life is so strong that the impact on those who encounter them (much like radioactive force) leaves a wake that cannot be undone.

Declaration

I will give you a new heart and put a new spirit in you; I will remove from you your heart of stone and give you a heart of flesh (Ezekiel 36:26, NIV).

Questions

What do you feel has the most power over your life? (e.g., your finances, time, relationships, opinions of others/approval)

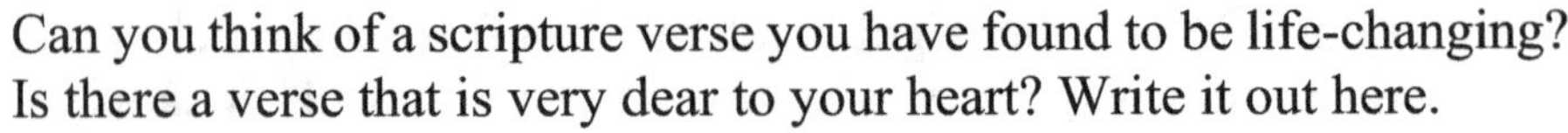

Can you think of a scripture verse you have found to be life-changing? Is there a verse that is very dear to your heart? Write it out here.

Why is the verse you chose above so meaningful? What power has it had in your life? What changes have you seen in your life from allowing this verse to infiltrate your heart?

Is there an area in your life where you need a verse to speak to your situation? Which situation is it? Take a moment to look up verses for this area in your life and write them below. Read them aloud and let them soak into your mind and soul.

Prayer

Thank you, Jesus, that there is no force in the universe stronger than you. You created every part of me. You know me. You know what I need. Please speak to my heart right now.

Take one minute to sit quietly and let God speak to you. Write down what he is saying to you.

Day 9:
Connected to the Source

One spring I decided to plant sunflowers in my backyard. When sunflowers are young, the stalks are very thin. I didn't have them staked for support because my ideal form of gardening is one where I invest minimal effort beyond a trip to the greenhouse.

A wild windstorm tore through one day that year. It ripped shingles off my house and it snapped the stalk of one of my sunflowers.

I left the sunflower laying there across the dirt because (you may recall) I don't actually put that much effort into my garden.

A few weeks later I was out in my garden when I noticed that the sunflower stem had shot up and continued to grow from the broken stalk. Though the stem was still broken, the stalk adjusted itself and from the breakage it grew upwards toward the sun.

You see, a broken sunflower can survive as long as the fibres of the stem remain attached and connected to the root system.

I don't know about you, but when storms in life inevitably come along, I hope that my fibres are strong enough to keep me connected to a solid root system. I want my connection to the source that gives me life to be strong enough to survive the storm. Even if I snap in half.

But there are times when I am sure my fibres have disconnected because I have been too busy to stay connected. Or, I have let pride get in my way and I trusted that I could do everything on my own better than I could with God. I didn't need a storm to sever my connection. I cut the whole stalk myself.

Romans 11:22-24 says,

> Consider therefore the kindness and sternness of God:

> sternness to those who fell, but kindness to you, provided that you continue in his kindness. Otherwise, you also will be cut off. And if they do not persist in unbelief, they will be grafted in, for God is able to graft them in again. After all, if you were cut out of an olive tree that is wild by nature, and contrary to nature were grafted into a cultivated olive tree, how much more readily will these, the natural branches, be grafted into their own olive tree! (NIV).

Jesus will not force himself on us. If we uproot ourselves from him and sever ourselves from his love with a lack of faith and trust, then he will allow us to do so. But through our faith and our trust in him, he is able to reconnect us.

If you feel like my broken sunflower or as though you have been pruned from God's tree of life, remember that he is a faithful gardener with more skills than I have and he is waiting to lovingly graft you back in.

So, let us strengthen the fibres that connect us to the root system. Let us do that before the storm comes. That though we make break, we are strong enough that we are not disconnected.

"We are hard pressed on every side, but not crushed; perplexed, but not in despair; persecuted, but not abandoned; struck down, but not destroyed" (2 Corinthians 4:8-9, NIV).

A breaking point will not be the end of you. It will be the start of a new upward journey if you are connected to the source that is Jesus. Day in and day out a sunflower needs so much from its roots. Are we to expect that we won't need the same?

If you were to cut a sunflower to bring into your home you would need to put it in a vase full of water to keep it alive. If you are really dedicated, you might give it some plant food. It can survive for a while not connected to the root system, but not for long. We too can function disconnected from our source of life for a while. But ultimately, we will not have the fulfilling promises of Jesus in our lives by using a substitution for an authentic life-giving source. This world offers many distractions and alternatives to Jesus. But none of them lead to the fullness of life in Christ except for a life in Christ.

Staying connected in scripture and in conversation and relationship with God will prevent that breaking point from being our end. The breakage will be our new beginning. A new stalk will keep growing up. By the end of the season, my broken sunflower bore just as beautiful a flower as the ones that did not snap. By the same small and unnoticeable changes that allowed that to happen, you will grow again too.

Declaration

I am the vine; you are the branches. If you remain in me and I in you, you will bear much fruit; apart from me you can do nothing (John 15:5, NIV).

Questions

In what part of your life do you feel most disconnected from God? (e.g., marriage, children, friendships, identity)

Can you list 2-3 practical steps you can take in the next week to begin to establish reconnection in each of the areas you listed?

Prayer

Write a prayer to God asking him to reconnect you in the areas where you need it. When you have finished writing this prayer, sit for 30 seconds and just listen for his response. Write down what the Holy Spirit reveals to you in this time.

Day 10: Incubation Period

When I was in my mid-twenties, I did a month-long backpacking trip through Europe. I stayed in some pretty sketchy hostels to save a few bucks along the way, but thought nothing of it. However, about six weeks after I got home, I noticed that I was getting tired very easily and getting frequent headaches. I chalked it up to being in a busy season of life and carried on feeling slightly unwell. But eventually it was clear that I was actually sick.

At first, I tried to deny it and make excuses for the symptoms. But towards the end of a particularly bad week, I found myself in a doctor's office admitting I was ill. After a blood test to confirm, I got the diagnosis: mononucleosis.

I learned then that mono has an incubation period of about 4-6 weeks before a person starts experiencing any symptoms. So, for almost six weeks after I got home, I was carrying this virus with me and I didn't know it.

I wonder what types of spiritual sickness, lies of the enemy, or sins we carry around with us unknowingly? Just like I was unaware that mono was infiltrating my body, I know there are spiritual illnesses in my life that are harmful but have yet to reveal themselves.

These could be sins that I am committing that do not make me feel the sting of death yet "For the wages of sin is death" (Romans 8:23a, NIV). It could be not making time for a close relationship with Jesus. Or, I may be allowing lies of the enemy to destroy my confidence, my relationships, my marriage or my peace. But right now, the pieces of my life remain largely intact.

In Psalm 139:23-24, David pens these words: "Search me, God, and know my heart; test me and know my anxious thoughts. See if there is any offensive way in me, and lead me in the way everlasting" (NIV).

Taking an inventory of our hearts allows us to identify areas where spiritual sickness is starting to take hold before we see the full-blown result in our lives. Just like I can be carrying around a physical illness for weeks without knowing it, I could also carry around a spiritual sickness before it makes me truly unwell. I do not want to wait until I feel "sick" before I begin to heal my spiritual walk. I've spent way too much time in my life ignoring the symptoms or making excuses for them, like I did when I tried to brush off my fight with mono.

I can insist that what I watch on TV isn't harming me, the feeds I scroll through do not pollute my thoughts, the people I hang out with are not leading me away from Jesus, or not spending time in God's Word has not impacted my relationship with him. The excuses can work and seem justified. For a time, anyway.

Will our spiritual health be like a physical sickness where we wait until we have debilitating symptoms before we take the time to get better? Or can we align our hearts with Jesus' day after day and allow him to search our hearts and find the things that are leading us astray and instead be led towards him?

As recorded in John 5:1-15 (NIV), Jesus encounters a man at the pool of Bethesda who is unable to walk. He had been sick for 38 years.

Jesus asked the man, "'Do you want to get well?'" (6)

Dear friend, Jesus is asking you if you want to get well, too. Really, truly, well in all areas of your life.

The interaction between Jesus and the man continues.

"'Sir,' the invalid replied, 'I have no one to help me into the pool when the water is stirred. While I am trying to get in, someone else goes down ahead of me.'" (7)

He begins with excuses and blames others for his lack of wellness. We all have excuses. I've blamed my kids, my commitments, and even my past circumstances for areas of my life where I have not allowed God to mend my heart. Excuses or not, Jesus still healed the man.

"'Get up! Pick up your mat and walk.'" (8)

We really need to allow Jesus to heal our spiritual hearts just as we ask him to heal us physically. After all, Jesus is a healer of our hearts and of our bodies.

We do not need to wait 38 years to be healed like the man who did not know Jesus. We do not need to wait until our spiritual illness has knocked us completely down either.

Can we begin to sit daily with God and reposition our hearts toward him? Can we re-focus our eyes on him so that we do not become spiritually unwell in the first place? Or, so that he can to begin to heal what already needs his restoration?

We can begin to walk out spiritually healthy lives before the things of this world pollute our spiritual health. And yet, if you find yourself beside a metaphorical pool waiting for Jesus to save you from an illness you already have, rest assured that excuses of the past are no longer relevant. Jesus is the ultimate healer of both our physical bodies and our spiritual lives.

Declaration

Because through Christ Jesus the law of the Spirit who gives life has set you free from the law of sin and death (Romans 8:2, NIV).

Questions

Has there been a time in your life when you felt like you ignored something going on in your heart and hoped that it would go away? What ended up happening? Did things get worse or better?

Is there anything in your heart right now that you know you should resolve before it becomes overwhelming? (e.g., unforgiveness, bitterness, jealousy) Write it down and be very specific. What happened? How did it make you feel then? How does it make you feel now?

Prayer

Write a prayer to God about the area of your life that you wrote about needing resolution for. Ask Him to lead you through healing, forgiveness, and restoration. Think about your answer to the first question. Is there is anything left to take to God in that situation? Write out a second prayer to help God begin to bring healing to that area as well.

Day 11:
Plant a Sycamore

When we built our home 13 years ago, we had to landscape our yard. Trees are expensive! So, we planted a few for privacy, but none that would grow big enough to provide us with any shade. There are so many days now that I can't get my umbrella to block the sun on my deck just right. I long to sit on the grass in the shade, but there is none. My husband and I often think we should have realized that some day down the line we might want a shady spot in our yard for warm summer days. But we did not think about it that way at the time. And now we have a hot deck and our grass gets scorched in the hot summer sun.

I've looked into it: you can buy a fairly big tree, but it's expensive. It would have made more sense to plant a small one 13 years ago. Not to mention, we would have had some shade for those 13 years while it grew.

There is an old saying that goes, "The best time to plant a tree was 20 years ago. The second-best time is today."

I still haven't planted any new trees. However, my tree situation got me thinking about a man named Zacchaeus.

When Jesus rolled into town, Zacchaeus wanted to see who he was. But unfortunately for Zacchaeus, he was short and he could not see over the crowd. Luke 19:4-5 says, "So he ran ahead and climbed a sycamore-fig tree to see him, since Jesus was coming that way. When Jesus reached the spot, he looked up and said to him, 'Zacchaeus, come down immediately. I must stay at your house today.' So he came down at once and welcomed him gladly" (NIV).

We won't ever know how or when that tree got planted there. But it could easily have been a few decades old. Without that tree, would Zacchaeus have been able to see Jesus when he arrived?

There are seeds that you need to be planting in your life right now. There are trees that you might need to have in your life years from now that you may not need today. Opening your Bible and spending those few minutes close to God can seem small and insignificant. But so was every single day of growth for that sycamore tree.

I am sure people walked by that sycamore tree day after day barely noticing little changes in it as it grew. But one day, that sycamore was so big and so strong that it held a sinner up high enough so Jesus could save him.

In Matthew 13:31-32 (NIV) Jesus mentions another type of tree.

"He told them another parable: 'The kingdom of heaven is like a mustard seed, which a man took and planted in his field. Though it is the smallest of all seeds, yet when it grows, it is the largest of garden plants and becomes a tree, so that the birds come and perch in its branches.'"

From small beginnings, a mustard seed grows to be the largest of garden plants. The small and insignificant act of planting a seed can yield so much growth! So much in fact that the tree becomes a shelter for the birds. It is from humble beginnings that these trees begin to grow into something useful.

So open your Bible. Spend time with God. Start the daily conversations. Learn more about his Word. Tiny steps day after day.

Because then eventually, there it is. A strong and mighty tree. After years of roots growing deep and branches growing tall, the tree becomes a shelter. Its roots go deep so that no wind or rain will wash it away, and its branches grow tall so that it may be a place for the birds to find a home, for a sinner to climb high enough to see Jesus, and even to provide shade for my back yard.

What you start today matters. 20 years will come and go no matter if you plant the seed or not.

Plant the seed.

Declaration

But I am like an olive tree flourishing in the house of God; I trust in God's unfailing love for ever and ever (Psalm 52:8, NIV).

Questions

What seeds which have been previously planted in your life that are now fully grown today? What were those small decisions or investments? What have they become now?

Are there seeds that you wish that you planted previously so that they could be fully grown now? Do you have your own version of that sycamore tree or mustard plant you wish you had in your life now, but do not?

What gift would you like to send to yourself 20 years from now? What can you do now that 20-years-from-now you would be thankful for? What specific seed can you plant today?

Prayer

Write a prayer asking God to show you where he wants to grow a full tree from a little seed in your life today. If you know what you really want to see the fruit of 20, 30, or 40 years from now, write a prayer asking God to show you the next step to keep building towards that.

Day 12:
A Slight Change in Course

After graduating from university, I decided to attend a small rural Bible school nestled in the province of Småland, Sweden. Coming from a big city and university life, it was a very difficult adjustment to a slower pace with very few things to do. However, the area was rich with lush forests to explore. Even within this slow and peaceful setting, God still taught me big lessons. Many of them were not taught within the classroom walls.

When you're from a city, there is something unnerving about hiking alone in the forest. The quietness feels unnatural. But I was ready to embrace this new lifestyle and I bravely set out to hike the area behind the school by myself, staying on the trails. My comfort level grew the more I explored and one day I decided that I would meander off the path and do some extra exploring in a heavily wooded area.

Eventually after a nice walk and some solid quiet time to myself, I was ready to start making my way back to school. I pointed myself towards where (I believed) the school was located and started walking back. I kept walking, but I couldn't find the school. I just saw more and more trees in front of me. I started to wonder if I had gotten turned around. Panic started to set in. I realized I didn't know what hungry Swedish animals I might encounter.

Finally, I spotted a familiar face in the bush. Another student was outside having a solo campfire. I ran up to him, panicked.

"I am so glad I found you!" I cried. "I am so lost!"

He chuckled at my situation and pointed me in the direction of the road that would take me back to the school.

When I eventually stumbled onto the road and figured out how far I still had to walk to get back to the school, I realized that I had pointed myself only slightly off course and missed the school by about 1/3 of a kilometer.

A slight deviation off course over a long enough period in time, and you are way off from where you intended to be.

There are a lot of things in life that are like that.

A few extra calories in a day and suddenly we are 10 lbs. above our ideal weight.

We spend a bit more than we make each month, and eventually we are drowning in debt.

We choose to neglect important relationships, and before we know it we have drifted apart.

And there's a big obvious one: we avoid reading our Bible regularly and end up further from God than we intended.

It's nothing big. We just skip a day here and there because we need to sleep in or new plans come up. But when we neglect God's Word for long enough, we suddenly realize that although we thought we were headed to the safety of God's shelter over our lives, we are actually in the wilderness feeling lost and frightened.

For a portion of my journey back towards the school, I was headed in the wrong direction, but I was still having my peaceful afternoon quiet time and didn't know. We can be off course, and we can still be at peace. For about 10-15 minutes, being misdirected was just part of the adventure for me. It took me a while to realize I hadn't arrived where I planned to be.

We may not necessarily know that we are off track at all until it's too late and we realize we are lost.

I don't want to be lost. There was a horrible feeling in the pit of my stomach when reality set in that I was in fact not where I thought I was.

This happened many years ago, so I didn't have the luxury of a map on my phone with a bright blue dot showing me exactly where I was.

Spiritually speaking though, we do have a blue dot of sorts. We have a Bible full of direction, guidance, wisdom, and help to keep us on the right path. If I am quick to pull out my phone to see where I am physically, then I need to be as quick to pull out my Bible to check where I am spiritually.

Just like I should have pointed myself towards the school and headed straight back, I need to open my Bible to point myself towards Jesus. If we spend time in the Word of God, we are not going to wander off. We won't be in the wilderness alone struggling to find our way back.

When we take the time to saturate our soul with the Word of God, we are trusting that his Word will carry us through this life even though at times we do not know where we are or where we are supposed to be going.

"Trust in the Lord with all your heart and lean not on your own understanding; in all your ways submit to him, and he will make your paths straight" (Proverbs 3:5-6, NIV).

We do not want to be so far off course that we struggle to find our way back and realize too late we have wandered off course and are lost and alone. I am so lucky that God allowed me to run into a fellow student that day. If you feel lost in the wilderness and don't quite know the way back, God is going to provide a way if you ask Him. Like my friend in the bush, Jesus is waiting for you to ask him for directions back home.

The Word of God is like a map to connect you back to God. You won't be caught off guard alone in the wilderness when you have the Word of God tucked into your heart. You will know who you are, whose you are, and where you are going.

Declaration

See, I am doing a new thing! Now it springs up; do you not perceive it? I am making a way in the wilderness and streams in the wasteland (Isaiah 43:19, NIV).

Questions

Does your relationship with God feel more like you are wandering lost in the woods hoping to make it to your destination, or does it feel like you are navigating with a map? How do you know if you are lost or if you are on the right path?

How would you know if you are lost? What safeguards do you have set in place to tell you when you have wandered off from your relationship with God? (e.g., Do you have a friend or family member who holds you accountable?)

How can you better navigate staying on course with God?

Prayer

Write a prayer asking God to help you identify the areas that distract you and lead you off course. Then as he reveals those areas, sit with them and write a prayer asking God help you avoid those detours.

Day 13:
Target Fixation

One cold winter day, I needed to quickly run into the city to pick up a Christmas gift for my son. I usually take a narrow back road to get there because as long as the weather is good, it's the quickest and easiest way to make that trip. As I turned onto the road, the conditions were not bad. However, as I kept driving, I noticed a car in the ditch. The conditions seemed fine to me, but I supposed it was possible that if someone was not driving to the weather they could have slid off the road.

I quickly grabbed the gift from the online pickup and immediately headed back home on the same road. To my surprise, in that short amount of time three other cars had hit the ditch. The road conditions were still not terrible.

I have noticed that sometimes on winter days when one car ends up in the ditch, others inevitably follow soon after. In fact, there is a phenomenon, known as target fixation, that explains this. It happens when someone is focused so hard on something (even to avoid it!) that they drive straight towards it (Jenkins, 2024).

On that wintery day, people driving by became so fixated on not hitting the ditch that some of them actually did!

This isn't the only time I have seen this. Believe me, I get frightened when my husband sees an animal way off on the other side of the road and suddenly the car starts to veer in that direction!

And of course it happens to me too. Not long ago, I picked up our brand-new car. When I was in my early twenties, I had accidently hit the curb with my parents' brand-new car and completely damaged one of the tire rims. For that reason, I was nervous about doing this with my own new car. As I pulled in to do my first school pickup with my new ride, my mind went, "Don't hit the curb! Don't hit the curb!" Suddenly, boom! I hit the curb! Never have I done this in years of pickups and drop-offs. But because I was so focused on the curb this one time, I hit it.

If target fixation happens with the direction our vehicles travel, what about the direction of the rest of our lives? Where we are looking is where we are going to end up. It will happen with our spiritual lives as easily as it does with our cars. If we are constantly eyeing up bigger, newer, fancier things, we will find a way to attain those things.

If we are focusing on our careers, then we will spend our time and energy finding ways to climb the ladder.

Or maybe we are focusing only on our own pleasures and comfort.

Our time and energy will go where we are looking.

Thankfully, this also means that if we are focusing on Jesus, we will find ourselves at his feet.

There are many things that are good, healthy, acceptable, and practical to strive for in life. And there is nothing wrong with owning possessions we value or having successful careers, positive life experiences, and achievements. But is the pursuit of bigger, better, newer, fancier, more prestigious, more successful, more exciting, and more popular all we are looking towards? Are we aiming into the ditch without even realizing it?

We spend so much time chasing things that are fleeting. Things that leave us drowning in debt or still wanting more. We focus so much of our life and energy on things that we leave on Earth when we die. We chase after what we cannot take with us into heaven. We sacrifice the eternal for the temporal. We look into the ditch to feel satisfied when there is so much more on the road ahead.

We cannot expect to stay on the road if we do not have our eyes focused on the road.

In Hebrews 12:1-2, Paul says, "Therefore, since we are surrounded by such a great cloud of witnesses, let us throw off everything that hinders and the sin that so easily entangles. And let us run with perseverance the race marked out for us, fixing our eyes on Jesus, the pioneer and perfecter of faith" (NIV).

There are things in our lives we need to get rid of if we are going to make time for Jesus. There are things that are entangling us. Things drawing our attention away from Jesus. We are spending our limited time and energy on that which has no eternal value and it is leading us into the ditch. We have things we will need to throw off to keep our focus on the road ahead.

Those cars in the ditch that winter day had to wait for a tow truck to come and haul them out. Staying on the road and staying focused in the first place is so much easier. Just like those drivers, if we don't take our eyes off Jesus, we won't skid off the road.

Declaration

But my eyes are fixed on you, Sovereign Lord; in you I take refuge—do not give me over to death (Psalm 141:8, NIV).

Questions

Make a list of all the thoughts that are stealing your attention away from God. They can be fears, insecurities, doubts. They can also be good, practical things, but they are taking attention away from Jesus nonetheless.

What does focusing on Jesus on a day-to-day basis look like for you?

Prayer

Write a prayer to God asking him to help you fixate your thoughts on him. Ask him to show you the areas of your life that you are focused on that are not leading you towards him.

Day 14:
Fashion and Transformation

It was 2014 and the time had come for me to trade in my out of style knee-high boots for some cute and fashionable ankle boots. An easy transition for some people, but I was confused by how I was supposed to style my jeans with the new boots.

It was clear the fashion rules indicated not to tuck your skinny jeans into the boots and instead cuff them. I scoured photos on Pinterest and fashion blogs to make sure I had the length right. I ended up having to buy a new pair of jeans to go with the new boots. Eventually I was ready to make my updated fashion debut, convinced I had it correct now.

It is easy enough to look around and see what is acceptable for fashion. Trends change more quickly than I can keep up with! But when it comes to my spiritual life and my walk with God, looking at trends and analyzing what everyone else is doing before trying it myself is not a wise idea. Updating our outfits with fashionable boots is not the same as the life-changing work that God wants to do on your heart through a personal relationship with him. Boots do not provide life-long confidence and assurance. The ankle-boot-skinny-jean trend didn't last. But confidence in oneself and God never goes out of style.

Romans 12:2 instructs us, "Do not conform to the pattern of this world, but be transformed by the renewing of your mind. Then you will be able to test and approve what God's will is—his good, pleasing and perfect will" (NIV).

We won't find our confidence by conforming to the pattern of this world. We cannot put ourselves together by copying what others around us are doing and presenting ourselves a certain way. Peace and transformation were never meant to be found by looking outside ourselves!

We feel that ache in our souls. Something is not right WITHIN us.

Peace and transformation are found by letting God work in our hearts. His Word is transformational. Relationship with him allows your heart and soul to interact with our world confidently.

It is easy to put on a cute outfit, walk into church, and act like we have it together and Jesus has changed our hearts. It is much harder to do the work to allow Jesus to change our hearts. Real transformation is not easy. For starters, our hearts are deceitful. Our nature is sinful. Ask anyone who has ever done any healing. It takes time and hard work. The answer isn't found by looking at someone else and copying them.

Transformation is not going to be found in looking the part. Jesus wants you to BE the part. You can wear the boots correctly and still not have your heart put together correctly. In this world, influencers and social media content dominate our lives. We constantly take in more airbrushed life than reality. What we see is often how we measure our value and meaning. And yet, we are still not satisfied with seeing perfection and trying to copy it. We constantly look to see how we measure up against standards that are not even real, against people who cannot give our hearts the wholeness they crave. We keep adjusting ourselves to hit closer to that mark.

Instead of merely adjusting our outfits to feel whole and secure, it is the work Jesus does in our hearts after spending time with him day after day that will make us healthy and confident. We don't need a filter. We don't need fancy lighting or the right algorithm to present ourselves fully to the world. We bring forth his light into the world. You will illuminate a room not with a fancy outfit, but simply because people will perceive that you have been in the presence of God.

"Do not lie to each other, since you have taken off your old self with its practices and have put on the new self, which is being renewed in knowledge in the image of its Creator" (Colossians 3:9-10, NIV).

Do not lie to and be fake with yourself any longer. Don't hide under new boots or a fancy outfit or a filter on your camera. You can find a new self in the knowledge of God. Dig into his Word. There is freedom there. You can find your true identity. Your confidence. There is fullness and there is a posture that you can rock that never goes out of style.

Declaration

Therefore, if anyone is in Christ, the new creation has come: The old has gone, the new is here (2 Corinthians 5:17, NIV)!

Questions

Has there ever been a situation or time when you felt your inside heart didn't match your outside persona? How did that feel?

What makes you feel confident and unapologetically yourself? Why do you think it makes you feel that way?

What does God need to do in your heart to allow you to become more confident from the inside and not just on the outside?

Prayer

Write a prayer asking God to transform you in the area you mentioned in the first question above.

Day 15:
Bending Toward the Light

I have a plant shelf in my dining room against the window. Having plants became a hobby of mine after my kids got a bit older. Since I kept my kids alive, maybe I was qualified to try house plants now! I've had a few successes and a few failures along the way. I've had to learn to water them on the right schedule depending on how much sun they get at a particular time of year. I've had to reposition a few of them in different locations around the house to try to save them. But sometimes even when the plants mostly thrive, they are a little off balance.

No matter where I position them in my house, only half of each plant is facing where the sun is coming through the window. Without fail, the plants grow sort of lopsided. They are not fully symmetrical with equal fullness on both sides. The plants begin to grow towards the light.

Bending toward the light allows plants to maximize photosynthesis and is called phototropism. Photoreceptive cells called phototropins allow the cells on the shaded side of the plan to swell, which ultimately causes the plant to bend towards the light (Trueman, 2023).

What a beautiful survival mechanism.

Even plants know to grow towards the light, not the darkness.

I am not sure I always lean in the direction of light. But like plants, I need a certain type of light so that I can grow too.

In John 8:12 Jesus declared, "I am the light of the world. Whoever follows me will never walk in darkness, but will have the light of life" (NLT).

When our lives become filled with endless social media distractions, Netflix, and busyness, we aren't getting the type of light necessary for growth.

We have become so accustomed to bending towards the darkness to get us through life. But darkness isn't life-giving.

We need to recognize the parts of ourselves that are leaning into darkness and shift those parts towards the light. But we have to do this ourselves, because we don't have phototropins.

It will take work. If part of you is feeling like it is in darkness, you will need to adjust your positioning.

In the movie A League of Their Own, Tom Hanks says, "It's supposed to be hard. If it were easy, everyone would do it."

There is no easy answer to how you make these adjustments in your life to let the light in. The allure of darkness and its distractions is a dopamine hit we crave. We can't stay away unless we work at it. To keep my plants alive took work. To keep my kids alive has taken work too. But at least kids scream at you when they are hungry! Plants just wither and die. And so does our spiritual life if we are not careful. One day you will notice that your faith has completely dried up while you weren't paying attention, just like that plant in the corner that completely dried up and died without ever letting you know that it needed care.

Adjust your life to let the light in. If your first adjustment doesn't work, then adjust again. Do not give up. Sometimes the third place I put a houseplant is finally the spot where it thrives. I don't know what will work for you, because YOU are the only one who can figure that out! But start the process of bending towards the light and see what happens in your life.

Declaration

The light shines in the darkness, and the darkness can never extinguish it (John 1:5, NLT).

Questions

What are the biggest things adding darkness to your life right now?

How can you add more light into your day-to-day life? (See the appendix for ideas.)

Prayer

Heavenly Father, I thank you that you want to add light to my life. Help me to see what is life-giving and what is actually turning life into death without me realizing it. If there is an area of my life that needs to change or something that I need to let go of or pick up, I pray that you would reveal that to me. Amen.

Day 16:
Hogan's Alley

When I was a child, I had a video game for my Nintendo called Hogan's Alley. It had a plastic gun accessory that you used to shoot your screen, and it somehow magically knew with precision if you hit the target.

In one of the Hogan's Alley games, the screen would move through a town and at each building either criminals or innocent bystanders would pop out from behind the building or in the windows. You needed to be a sharpshooter to hit the criminals before they disappeared as quickly as they appeared. However, you needed to be careful not to shoot the civilians that popped up just as quickly. You needed to shoot fast, but you also had to quickly identify who was bad and who was good.

Now that I'm grown up, I realize my spiritual journey is much like the game of Hogan's Alley. I often have bad thoughts, evil accusations, or attacks from the enemy jump out at me like the bad guys in my video game, in between the words of truth that I try to live my life by. But unlike the game, I don't even take half a second to identify each thought as one of the "good guys" or "bad guys". And I definitely don't shoot down the "bad guys" the same way I would an animated villain.

Our lives would look very different if we were alert and ready to take out the bad thoughts, lies, and untruths the enemy uses to take us down. After all, our lives are much more important than a Nintendo game! The Bible says that there is no truth in the devil and that he is the father of lies. When he speaks, there is no truth in him (John 8:44). Lies are his weapon. We are not fighting cartoon bad guys with a little plastic Nintendo gun aimed at a TV. But we do have insecurities, doubts, regrets, and shame that jump out of hiding. We have a real enemy (even if we cannot see him) and our weapons are more than some strange technology from the 1980s. We have real power to take down the evil that is trying to destroy us.

> "For though we live in the world, we do not wage war as the world does. The weapons we fight with are not the weapons of the world. On the contrary, they have divine power to demolish strongholds. We demolish arguments and every pretension that sets itself up against the knowledge of God, and we take captive every thought to make it obedient to Christ" (2 Corinthians 10:3-5, NIV).

These weapons we fight with are the words of God. This is a battle. We need to have the armour of God, but it isn't enough to just suit up. We also have powerful weapons available to us which we need to use.

"Take the helmet of salvation and the sword of the Spirit, which is the word of God" (Ephesians 6:17, NIV).

Fighting our enemy with the words of God may feel insufficient. However, we've all tried to use our own words to fight. It may have started when we were children, fighting with a sibling or a friend using name calling or tattling. Then we became adults and progressed to tweeting our opinions and our passive aggressive comments. We may have resorted to manipulation or using our words to control people or situations around us.

As humans, we already fight with words. Let's use the Word of God to take out the REAL enemy.

The Word of God is the only true weapon. But we need to actually have the Word of God within us to do this.

For the Word of God is alive and active. "Sharper than any double-edged sword, it penetrates even to dividing soul and spirit, joints and marrow; it judges the thoughts and attitudes of the heart" (Hebrews 4:12, NIV).

I've never seen a social media comment or argument with words that are that powerful.

So, back to Hogan's Alley. While we are not training to be FBI agents in need of firing practice, to win our spiritual battle we need to discern truth from lies. We can do this by familiarizing ourselves with truth.

When the lies of the enemy jump out at us, we need to identify them quickly and take them down.

The battle plan is this: first, we need to know the Word of God. This is like playing Hogan's Alley and knowing that gangsters and bank robbers are bad and the professor and the lady with a baby are good. We need to open our Bible and actually read it. We need to meditate on it. When something speaks to us personally, we need to take the time to let that sink into our lives. We need to internalize this weapon so that we may use it externally. This is how we prepare ourselves.

Secondly, we need to filter our lives through the Word of God. Like putting on prescription glasses to see clearly, we need to take the Word of God and view life through that lens and perspective. We need to ask God for discernment in our lives when things are unclear to us. The more truth we have tucked into our hearts, the easier it will be to identify the ways in which the enemy is trying to take us down. This is the quick reflex that tells us we see a "bad guy" when we see the bank robber on the screen.

Lastly, just like in Hogan's Alley, once we know that we are dealing with a lie we have to take the shot. Shoot God's truth at the lie. Use the Word of God as your ammunition. The enemy knows that if we know truth but we do not fight with truth, then our knowledge does not matter. "Do not merely listen to the word, and so deceive yourselves. Do what it says" (James 1:22, NIV).

Walk through your day-to-day life aware that an enemy prowls, ready to destroy you. For example, you might hear a soft whisper in your mind that says, "You aren't enough." This voice whispers so quietly that you might not even detect it unless you are aware of the schemes of the devil. With the Word of God in your heart and a firm understanding of the weapons your enemy is using to hurt you, you are not going to accept such an accusation or lie. You have the Word of God as your armour and your weapon. Even an inkling of doubt or the smallest of lies engages your arsenal of truth. These lies will keep popping up around corners unexpectedly, just like the bank robbers and gangsters, but by spending time in God's Word day after day you are now packing some serious divine heat.

Declaration

Finally, be strong in the Lord and in his mighty power. Put on the full armor of God, so that you can take your stand against the devil's schemes (Ephesians 6:10-11, NIV).

Questions

What are some lies you know are coming at you? List at least three different lies masquerading as if they are true statements about your worth or your identity.

Write out God's truth that contradicts each lie listed above. You may need to do a Bible keyword search to find each truth.

Prayer

Write a prayer to God asking him for his discernment over your thought life and your beliefs about yourself. Pray over each of the lies you listed above and ask God for his truth over all the lies. Take a moment to sit with Jesus in silence and listen to him speak truth over your heart. Write down anything that comes to you.

Day 17:
Fake It Till You Make It

After I finished high school, I went to university to get my Education degree. I was only 21 years old when I did my first teaching practicum and taught Grade 10 students who did not feel that much younger than me! There was a common phrase we used as student teachers: "Fake it till you make it!" It helped us get through those initial feelings of insecurity.

We might not have known what we were doing, but we were going to pretend we did.

When you begin to open your Bible and sit with Jesus, you might feel like this newfound spiritual person isn't really you.

But our character follows our actions.

I think of Jesus when he was inviting his disciples to follow him. These were not men who studied every day at the temple hoping to become religious leaders. He didn't say, "get all your biblical education and then come find me." Instead, Mark 1:16-18 records, "As Jesus walked beside the Sea of Galilee, he saw Simon and his brother Andrew casting a net into the lake, for they were fishermen. 'Come, follow me,' Jesus said, 'and I will send you out to fish for people.' At once they left their nets and followed him" (NIV).

Jesus said first to follow him, then he promised to make them fishers of men.

To become an experienced teacher, I had to first teach.

James 4:8 says, "Come near to God and he will come near to you" (NIV).

The Bible doesn't talk about waiting for Jesus to establish a relationship with him by sitting and doing nothing. Instead, it requires action on our behalf. It requires us to initiate.

When Jesus healed the man at the pool in Bethesda, he still instructed the man, "Stand up, pick up your mat, and walk!" (John 5:8, NLT). This man still needed to take that first step. Jesus wasn't going to do it for him.

To grow in our faith and experience the transforming power of Jesus in our lives we are going to need to take that first step. We are going to need to stand up. We are going to need to follow Jesus before we can become more like Jesus. He will transform us on the journey, not before it.

The man at the pool first had to stand and then walk before he was ever going to run.

You must live like you are a strong woman of God before you become a strong woman of God. You will have to make that your priority before it feels like it is the most important part of your day. Until it really feels like it, act like it is.

Feelings follow our actions.

Act like you are the daughter of a king. Move like you are headed straight into Jesus' arms even when you don't feel that way yet.

I have days when my feelings fluctuate. Some days I have more energy, some days I feel cranky, and other days I feel full of joy. But none of that changes the truth about who I am, where I want to be headed, and whose arms I want to head into.

So, each day I will live like I am headed towards Jesus. Each day I will follow Jesus and then I will slowly grow and become like the fishers of men.

We call it a walk with God because we are just taking one step at a time. That is all walking is: one step after another. But you have to take the first step to start walking.

Sit with God like the woman of God you desire to be. Then get ready for him to do more than you could ever ask or imagine.

Declaration

If you look for me whole heartedly, you will find me (Jeremiah 29:13, NLT).

Questions

Have you ever enjoyed something more after you started it? Maybe a sport? Or a TV show you got into after a few episodes? List some of the things that took you a while to get excited about.

Do you have ideas about the type of woman in Christ you would like to be? (e.g., more patient, forgiving, generous, a prayer warrior, more knowledgeable about scripture, bold, brave, courageous, unshakeable, etc.) List some of the ways you would like God to transform you.

Prayer

Write a prayer to God asking him to show you who he has created you to be. Ask him which areas in your life he wants to transform. Then, ask him to reveal to you the ways that you are created in his image.

Day 18:
Multiply

There is a word we glorify in our culture. That word is "busy". Ask anyone how they are, and they will usually respond with "busy!" like a badge of honour. Proof our lives have meaning and substance.

Busy does not mean productive. Busyness does not require intentionality. And busy does not guarantee victory.

I can't think of anyone whose life has more mission and purpose than the life of Jesus. His life and death split time as we measure it into BC and AD. His ministry lasted only three years. Stated another way, he only had three years to impact history for all time. But we read over and over again that Jesus "withdrew to lonely places and prayed" (Luke 5:16, NIV). He was no stranger to needing to make time for solitude with his father.

Jesus' time was limited. But his impact is endless.

Could our lives hold the same power? Our time is limited, but can our impact also be endless?

During those three years, the disciples were also very busy. Too busy even to eat at times! Mark 6:30-32 says,

> The apostles gathered around Jesus and reported to him all they had done and taught. Then, because so many people were coming and going that they did not even have a chance to eat, he said to them, 'Come with me by yourselves to a quiet place and get some rest.' So, they went away by themselves in a boat to a solitary place (NIV).

Many of us are very familiar with how this story continues. When they reached the shore, the people had arrived ahead of them. The busyness of their ministry did not let up. Jesus began teaching them. It grew late and there was no food for all these people to eat.

Mark 6:35-44 (NIV) records what happened next.

> By this time it was late in the day, so his disciples came to him. 'This is a remote place,' they said, 'and it's already very late. Send the people away so that they can go to the surrounding countryside and villages and buy themselves something to eat.'
>
> But he answered, 'You give them something to eat.'
>
> They said to him, 'That would take more than half a year's wages! Are we to go and spend that much on bread and give it to them to eat?'
>
> 'How many loaves do you have?', he asked. 'Go and see.'
>
> When they found out, they said, 'Five—and two fish.'

Then Jesus directed them to have all the people sit down in groups on the green grass. So they sat down in groups of hundreds and fifties. Taking the five loaves and the two fish and looking up to heaven, he gave thanks and broke the loaves. Then he gave them to his disciples to distribute to the people. He also divided the two fish among them all. They all ate and were satisfied, and the disciples picked up twelve basketfuls of broken pieces of bread and fish. The number of the men who had eaten was five thousand."

These men were busy with their ministry with Jesus. It must have been non-stop travelling, people brought to be healed, criticism and skepticism, rejection. They didn't even have a chance to eat. But they still took time to go into solitude, and then what happened next?

They gave Jesus what they had. Five loaves of bread and two fish. And Jesus multiplied it.

Jesus is only asking us for what we have. If all we have is five loaves of bread and two fish, then that is all he is asking us for. If all you have is one minute to sit and pray, or one minute to sit and listen, he will take that one minute and multiply it into something so much bigger.

The food they had was limited. But with Jesus, the food became unlimited.

Your time is finite. But with Jesus, your impact can become infinite.

You may not feel like you have enough, but with Jesus there is abundance.

We hoard the little we have. We don't offer it to God. We want to control 100% of our time, energy, and even our wealth.

Jesus and his disciples had to get into a boat and leave the shore for their solitude. This way of getting alone time just isn't practical for most of us. But if we don't have boats, we have cozy chairs. We have park benches. We can even hide for a few minutes in the pantry and pray.

If we want victories in our lives and we want purpose over busyness, we don't need to do more, we just need to give to Jesus what we have. He will do the rest.

Declaration

Give, and it will be given to you. A good measure, pressed down, shaken together and running over, will be poured into your lap. For with the measure you use, it will be measured to you (Luke 6:38, NIV).

Questions

What small things can you give to God? In other words, what are the loaves and fishes you have to bring to Jesus?

What is holding you back from giving what you have to Jesus?

Prayer

Write a prayer to God asking for help giving over what little you do have to him.

Day 19:
Rivers

When I was in my early twenties, I was a very new Christian. I loved church and Jesus, but I kept a foot in two different worlds and I tried to live between life abundantly with Jesus and the promises of fulfillment in this world.

My attempt did not work. I could not serve two masters. I ended up exhausted and depressed. My boyfriend dumped me. One of my closest friends at the time then ghosted me. The only two friends I had at church decided that they were no longer going to go there with me. When I look back on this time, every day seems etched in my mind like it was cloudy and cold. I don't remember sunshine. It was as if every day there was impending rain.

Thankfully, I decided to step fully into life with Jesus and stop straddling two worlds. But the hurt and the rejection remained as I took steps towards a life with Jesus. In that low place, I needed a lot of Jesus to move forward.

Revelation 22:1 says, "Then the angel showed me the river of the water of life, as clear as crystal, flowing from the throne of God and of the Lamb" (NIV).

There is a river flowing from the throne of God.

And, here is an obvious but interesting fact: rivers always flow downhill.

The beginning of a river is called its "source", where the current is strongest. And typically, this source would be a melting glacier, snow-covered mountains, or sometimes even a spring. The energy that causes a river to flow is gravity. Rainstorms can increase the current and add to its intensity. A river of water is a force that cannot be stopped. It just keeps directing itself downward, without end (Rutledge et al., 2023).

For example, the Grand Canyon was formed by the Colorado River cutting its way through the landscape of Arizona over a long period of time (Witze, 2019).

If you are at a low point right now, I want to remind you that our world has our creator's fingerprints all over it. He has painted a beautiful illustration of how much he wants his love to flow down from his throne into your life. Nothing will stop it.

"You make springs pour water into the ravines, so streams gush down from the mountains" (Psalm 104:10, NLT).

When I began making choices towards stepping fully into my faith even in the midst of the depression, the loss, the rejection, and redirection of my life, God came down to meet me there. However, things didn't change rapidly.

Just like the Grand Canyon, transformation took time. God sent his Son to save us in the form of a baby instead of a full-grown man because there is a process to all that he does. He uses time and the force of his love to erode away pain and deadness, transforming us into a mighty example of how God's Word penetrating our lives creates natural beauty that takes our breath away.

Just as a river with immense power can change an entire landscape, Jesus wants to change your life from a formless desert into a river valley full of abundant life by the force of his love.

There was a process of building my life with Jesus. Like a river, he had to carve a way through the hard places of my heart and my life. It involved finding friends and building relationships with those walking a similar journey. Investing my time and energy in my faith and learning the Word of God. Getting involved in church. Finding ways to serve.

Do not give up when the process takes a long time.

It's been almost 20 years since I walked through that cloudy period in my life. Perhaps those rain clouds encircling my life were simply God getting ready to unleash more rain and intensify the flow of his love poured down on me. Like a storm, he wanted to add to the intensity of the river he was using to change the landscape of my life.

He wants to do that in your life too. He is never done with you. Rivers never stop changing the landscape that they flow through. The same is true for the love of God.

Bring yourself close to God. Open up your Bible and take in his Word. Because the closer you are to the source, the stronger the river of love he pours out on you will be.

Declaration

Whoever believes in me, as Scripture has said, rivers of living water will flow from within them (John 7:38, NIV).

Questions

How has God already changed the landscape of your life? What are huge changes that he has made in your journey with him? (e.g., eye-opening discoveries or changes in your thought patterns, habits or lifestyle)

In what ways did God work those changes into your life?

How would you like God to change the landscape of your life right now? What does God need to chisel or etch away from your life?

Prayer

Write a prayer to God asking for him to carve a new future ahead. Surrender the areas that you know will be extra hard for him to carve a path through. Include in your prayer the ways that you are thankful and grateful for specific ways he has already made his love flow through your life.

Day 20:
Wedding Crashers

I attended a friend's wedding once where I only really knew the bride and a few of her bridesmaids. The table for the wedding reception was a group of people that my plus one and I did not know. We found our table and two men were already seated there. We began with the usual "What do you do?" questions to get to know each other and one of the men said that he was a doctor. My friend and her new husband were nurses, so I assumed that was the connection.

The two men were a bit older but had a seemingly solid connection to the bride and groom so we left it at that and the night continued on. Our table was having a great night visiting and sharing dinner together. After the speeches, it was finally time to get up and mingle with other tables. One of the bridesmaids I knew approached me immediately.

She inquired skeptically, "Who are those two guys at your table?"

"The one said he was a doctor," I replied. "But other than that, I don't really know."

The bridesmaid told me that everyone at the head table had been trying to decipher who the men could be. Suddenly, an idea clicked in her head.

"WEDDING CRASHERS!" she shrieked. She then proceeded to run them out the door.

We had a good laugh about it at the time.

Jesus spoke of a wedding in his parable of the ten virgins in Matthew 25:1-13:

> Then the Kingdom of Heaven will be like ten bridesmaids who took their lamps and went to meet the bridegroom. Five of them were foolish, and five were wise. The five who were

> foolish didn't take enough olive oil for their lamps, but the other five were wise enough to take along extra oil. When the bridegroom was delayed, they all became drowsy and fell asleep. At midnight they were roused by the shout, "Look, the bridegroom is coming! Come out and meet him!" All the bridesmaids got up and prepared their lamps. Then the five foolish ones asked the others, "Please give us some of your oil because our lamps are going out." But the others replied, "We don't have enough for all of us. Go to a shop and buy some for yourselves." But while they were gone to buy oil, the bridegroom came. Then those who were ready went in with him to the marriage feast, and the door was locked. Later, when the other five bridesmaids returned, they stood outside, calling, "Lord! Lord! Open the door for us!" But he called back, "Believe me, I don't know you!" (NLT).

The bridegroom in this parable is Jesus. Half the women were ready and half of them were not.

I think our tendency is to believe that we are most like the five who were wise and ready.

From the outside, the ten bridesmaids probably looked the same. They were all carrying lamps and dressed for a wedding. The difference was what was on the inside.

Five of them were not prepared and did not have any fuel for their lamps. And, their lack of effort and their laziness in drifting off to sleep meant that they were frantically trying to get ready when the bridegroom arrived.

I can feel like I am ready for the wedding. I can look around at those who are in my circle and I can feel good about them and where I am at in my walk with God. That comparison that says, "they're too busy to read their Bible too" makes me feel better. It allows me to look around and feel that I am as holy as the people next to me when my list of church activities is the same as that of my friends.

All the women were standing there with their lamps. But it was the ones who had the oil inside who were let in.

On our journey, we are continually measuring what we have and if we have enough. We ask ourselves if we are doing enough or if we ARE enough. How will we know when we have done enough church activities, listened to enough sermons, or sang enough worship songs?

In the parable, the women all wanted to be let in.

"'Lord, Lord', they cried. But he replied, 'Truly I tell you, I don't know you'" (Matthew 25:11-12, NIV).

It is not about looking like wedding guests. It's about who you know. It's about being ready. At the door, Jesus didn't ask for a list of church activities or inquire about church attendance.

The issue was whether the bridegroom knew them or not. These bridesmaids chose not to be ready. And his reply was, "Truly I tell you, I don't know you." Like the wedding crashers at my friend's wedding, it didn't matter that they were around when the wedding was happening. It didn't matter that they got to know a few people at one table. They weren't thrown out because they didn't know how to have a good time at a wedding. It didn't matter that they were polite dinner guests. The bride and the groom did not know them. And so, they were not allowed in.

The measure of being let in was what was on the inside. Our culture is so focused on what is on the outside, but we rarely consider what fuel we are carrying on the inside.

I haven't been a wedding crasher myself, but I have been to a wedding where I did not know the bride or groom. No matter how glamorous the celebration is, there is an element missing when you are a guest who only knows half the couple: the whole love story. I have been to many weddings where I knew the couple very well, and I knew their story because I had been along for it. The wedding where you hold back tears because you are so happy for both people is a glorious celebration. Jesus wants us to plan for the wedding by knowing the bridegroom personally. So we know the love story. Then we are truly the welcome guests.

Declaration

I want to know Christ—yes, to know the power of his resurrection and participation in his sufferings, becoming like him in his death, and so, somehow, attaining to the resurrection from the dead (Philippians 3:10, NIV).

Questions

How do you measure your spiritual health?

On a scale of 1 to 10 (10 being very close), how would you rate your closeness to Jesus today?

If you answered 1-5, can you think of a time in your life when it was closer to a 10? Why do you think you had a higher score then? What lead to that? If it is above 5, what would you say contributes to this higher number?

What is one thing you can do today to draw closer to God?

Prayer

Write a prayer to God asking him to show how you can get more fuel for your lamp. Ask God to lead you to a deeper connection with him. One where you can stand at the door and proclaim you know the bridegroom well.

Day 21:
Foundations

When we were engaged, my husband and I began the search for a home we would live in together after we got married. We found an empty lot that felt like a dream come true! So, instead of buying a home already built, we went through the nine-month-long process of picking out every last detail and waiting for it all to come together. It was a lot of work at a very busy time in our lives, but we still made the effort to visit the site every week and check on the construction progress of our home.

Finally, the day came that we went out to our lot and saw that they had finally poured the concrete foundation for our house. It was an exciting day!

Except for a tiny portion that sticks out one or two feet above ground before our siding begins, that foundation isn't visible to us anymore. We have a subfloor and carpet, and drywall, paint, and photos now cover the walls. We know it is there and it is strong enough to hold up the rest of the house. We do not see the foundation, but we see everything else the foundation holds in place.

The foundation of our home wasn't built with particle board or plastic. The foundation is made from concrete reinforced with rebar and it goes deep into the ground. If we don't cut corners or use cheap materials for our earthy homes, then why do I often allow things in my life to be built using unstable material, making for poor construction of my heavenly home?

Is my confidence built on the opinions of others?

Is my self-worth tied to the size of my paycheque or job title?

Instead, could Jesus Christ become the foundation of our confidence?

There is a sturdiness in our lives when we take the time to rest in the truth of scripture and build a relationship with Jesus as the foundation. A time will come when it will be revealed to us if we have built our lives with poor workmanship and cheap materials or whether we have solid construction.

1 Corinthians 3:12-15 says:

> If anyone builds on this foundation using gold, silver, costly stones, wood, hay or straw, their work will be shown for what it is, because the Day will bring it to light. It will be revealed with fire, and the fire will test the quality of each person's work. If what has been built survives, the builder will receive a reward. If it is burned up, the builder will suffer loss but yet will be saved—even though only as one escaping through the flames (NIV).

It is actually much easier for me to compromise and build the foundation of my life by cutting corners with quick fixes versus building a solid deep connection with Jesus than it would be for a builder constructing my home to cut corners by using inferior materials and shoddy workmanship. There are checks and balances in place to ensure builders complete their work to code and get inspections and proper permits. But in our spiritual lives we are willing to make tiny compromises that threaten the integrity on which our spiritual life will stand, and no one knows but us.

We make excuses to justify skipping Bible reading and praying. But perhaps on the day my home needed its foundation poured, the builders decided to list off their reasons for cutting corners that day. I am sure it is possible they had a difficult weekend, a fight with their spouse, money concerns on their mind, family issues to deal with, or kids tiring them out. These are some of the same excuses we use to cut corners in our spiritual lives! But the builders completed the work pouring my foundation to code regardless of how they felt at any given time when they were building my house. The quality was not built on feelings or circumstances, but on a commitment to do things properly for everyone's safety and wellbeing.

My home deserved to be built to last and withstand decades of life within its walls. The same is true for your soul.

I am not talking about needing a specific amount of time spent in God's Word. This is between you and God. Only the two of you know the strength and foundation of your faith.

About two years after we moved into our house, my husband and I were driving home in a huge storm. We couldn't see the road in front of us because the rain was pouring down so hard. When we turned onto our street, we did not see the huge lake that had formed right in our path. We drove our car straight into the flooded street. Our poor Jetta was half-sunk under water.

We jumped out of our now-submerged car windows and ran home. If the street was flooded, I dreaded seeing our house. I thought it must be under water by now. Our home backs onto a storm runoff pond, and I worried the water would reach our basement. We made it back to our house and opened the gate to our backyard. It was completely dark and I could not see anything as I walked further and further towards the pond in utter darkness, full of dread. I expected my feet to hit water, but I made it to the back fence and thankfully the water had not yet entered our yard. It was about three feet away from the fence. The ground would be saturated for days. But the foundation held. The weeping tile and sump pump did their jobs.

Modern-day homes do not wash away because we have engineered technology, standards, and accountability. But I ask again, do you keep your spiritual life to the same standard? Your life is more precious than a house. Your soul was built for eternity. We know activities like Bible study and prayer are life-giving, but we do not treat them or protect them as well as we do our possessions. We buy insurance in case an accident happens with our house. But what is our insurance policy for our spiritual life? Do we pay the premiums monthly for that protection? Or do we risk leaving that area of our life vulnerable?

> Therefore everyone who hears these words of mine and puts them into practice is like a wise man who built his house on the rock. The rain came down, the streams rose, and the winds blew and beat against that house; yet it did not fall, because it had its foundation on the rock. But everyone who hears these words of mine and does not put them into practice is like a

> foolish man who built his house on sand. The rain came down, the streams rose, and the winds blew and beat against that house, and it fell with a great crash (Matthew 7:24-27, NIV).

Treat your spiritual life better than your home. It will hold you for eternity. When the storms come, you need to be put together with the same strength that put together the whole universe.

Declaration

It is because of him that you are in Christ Jesus, who has become for us wisdom from God—that is, our righteousness, holiness and redemption (1 Corinthians 1:30, NIV).

Questions

What have you built your confidence and identity on? What makes you feel important, valued, special, loved?

Where do you feel God is calling you to increase your trust in him with holding the important pieces of your life together?

Where do you feel especially vulnerable in your relationship with God?

Prayer

Write a prayer asking Jesus to help you identify the areas of your spiritual foundation where you need his help increasing your strength.

Day 22:
Prepare for Battle

I joined a Bible study recently. While I knew I wanted to do something that was going to dig very deep into the Word of God, this particular study had more homework than I was expecting. The sheer amount I had to do actually made me feel too overwhelmed to even start. Then, distractions came piling in. Some distractions were just life circumstances we can't avoid, like my kids getting sick. But some were more spiritual than logistic. I would sit down to do my homework and my to-do list would whisper to me. My phone was luring me. I'd remember who I needed to text back, and that thing I needed to follow up on.

The devil wanted to make sure I didn't open my Bible. And when I did, he wanted to make sure I was overwhelmed. And if I started to go through the study, he wanted to distract me from being fully engaged.

It's an all-out war for our souls.

On the night Jesus was betrayed, he entered the Garden of Gethsemane and he said these words to his disciples: "My soul is crushed with grief to the point of death. Stay here and keep watch with me" (Matthew 26:38, NLT).

Keep watch.

Keep watch even when your soul is crushed. You have an enemy that wants to take you down. Little by little, so you don't notice it. It is easy to go through life always looking down. But we need to have our heads up and keeping watch.

"Be alert and of sober mind. Your enemy the devil prowls around like a roaring lion looking for someone to devour. Resist him, standing firm in the faith, because you know that the family of believers throughout the world is undergoing the same kind of sufferings" (1 Peter 5:8-9, NIV).

1 Peter 5:9 says we need to "resist him". This battle is not unique to you, although the enemy of your heart wants you to believe that it is.

Remember that nobody would try to steal from you that which isn't valuable. Nobody ever tries to steal the trash out of my garbage can, for example. So, if the enemy wants to keep me away from the Word of God, then perhaps that is a sign that I need to push into it even further. If the enemy is fighting against me, that means I must fight back harder. Whatever it is that might happen when I start to go through that Bible study, the enemy wants nothing more than to see it never come to fruition.

Bible reading, prayer, and devotional time is valuable. And the devil wants to steal them.

When these moments come into our lives and we feel like there is every reason not to push into God, then that is a pretty good sign the roaring lion has found something he knows is worth devouring. So, instead of giving in, what if we realized that we should actually then push in?

How powerful would a generation of women be who didn't put their Bibles down when they were in school, handling work deadlines, raising young children, or caring for aging parents? Of course, Satan wants you to believe that now is not the time for reading God's Word!

There will never be a perfect time to read God's Word. The time is now. Whatever your season. There is no season when time with Jesus is useless.

So, back to my Bible study homework. I sat at my kitchen counter one day staring at the blank, uncompleted pages. I decided to ask for God's help to focus and ignore the distractions:

"This Bible study is hard and the amount of work in it is overwhelming. But I am trusting that you have something incredible in this tough journey. I will not be afraid of how much work this is. Help me to find the time and discipline to keep pushing and keep working even when it isn't easy."

The distractions remained. At times I was unable to focus and had to say that prayer over again. But I kept fighting. Because I knew there was a battle and an enemy who wanted to take me down and convince me that I didn't have time for this, and I probably wouldn't get anything out of it anyway.

Every time you resist the nagging voice that tells you that you don't have time and that you should do everything else in the world but dig into God's Word, you are taking back ground from the enemy. Even one small step at a time is a battle won. Your enemy will never disappear. The distraction and excuses in this life will never stop coming at you. If you are waiting for the perfect time when this will be easier, hear me when I say that day won't ever come.

Take back ground. One prayer, one chapter, one Bible study, one song, one devotional at a time. Meditating on a verse. A moment of silence to hear God's voice without the distractions. These are fierce weapons. God's Word is alive and active (Hebrews 4:12). Pick up your weapon! You are in a battle. You are in a war.

Do not expect spending time with God to be easy. Anticipate the fight. Be prepared for battle.

Towards the end of Paul's life, he wrote these words to Timothy:

"I have fought the good fight, I have finished the race, I have kept the faith" (2 Timothy 4:7, NIV).

It is a fight, but it is a good fight. It is a worthwhile fight. Paul had no regrets.

Neither will you.

Declaration

The thief comes only to steal and kill and destroy; I have come that they may have life, and have it to the full (John 10:10, NIV).

Questions

What are your biggest distractions when it comes to God's Word?

When you sit down to spend time with God, what types of distractions or thoughts pop up? Do you find that you are focused during this time? Write down the lies that you may be hearing.

Prayer

Write a prayer asking God to show you the lies that the enemy is speaking to you and ask him to help you find your focus. Speak your prayer aloud so the enemy knows that you are taking back ground.

Day 23: Finding Comfort

I felt the floor drop out from under me. I was in free fall. Nothing holding me up. Gravity kept pulling me downwards. Nothing was going to make it stop it until I hit bottom. I didn't know whether to hold my breath or take a deep breath. Neither would stop the downward momentum. Then I opened my eyes and brought myself back to reality. I was just standing in my kitchen. I grounded myself in the moment. I had a meal to make for my kids. My free fall experience was only in an emotional sense. The choices of others had stolen so much from me. It felt as if the ground had been pulled out from underneath me, but only metaphorically. I still had to go about my day. Emptying the dishwasher, loading the washing machine. This was one of the worst weeks of my life. The loss I was facing felt like my undoing. But here I was, doing everything I had to do.

In the days prior, I had to walk away from a very toxic and abusive relationship with a family member after years of narcissistic abuse. Not only was the pain from what I endured so overwhelming, but the next steps towards healing felt excruciating in those first days as well.

People always act as though reading the Bible or connecting with Jesus would be that "one more thing" that would push them over the limit on their to-do list. I was falling apart. I had nothing left in me during that time. I desperately needed Jesus to calm my anxious heart and give me peace. I felt like I couldn't do this on my own strength, and I was right. I surrendered my ability to do it all on my own without putting Jesus first. I was desperate for the Word of God.

This particular week, and the months and even years that followed had some utterly heartbreaking moments. I didn't open my Bible out of obligation. I didn't do it to look like or even pretend that I felt like a good Christian girl. I did it because I had nothing left of my own. I needed sustenance that did not come from within me, but from outside of me.

Make no mistake, this season was horrific. I know you have walked times like this too. We crave comfort and goodness instead of the pain we are enduring. Spending time with Jesus really is one of the least applauded and sought after comforts of life. I did it because I needed goodness. In a world full of trouble, I needed a refuge. But Jesus is not necessarily the relief we run towards first.

Jesus wants us to delight ourselves in his Word (Psalm 37:4). He wants us to seek after him with the same passion we have when we seek after the comforts of this life.

He wants us to delight in him the way that we do a walk on the beach to watch the sunset. To appreciate the sound of Jesus' voice the way the sound of a beautiful song moves our soul. To find our contentment in him like we do when we spend time with friends who spark life in us. Jesus wants us to find pleasure in his Word the same way we experience joy in those other things. We seek those things because they fulfil our hearts and desires. He wants us to run to his Word because it equally overwhelms us with the same contentedness and satisfaction. We can seek his Word as one of the truest pleasures in this world.

The book of Psalms starts with these promising words:

> Blessed is the one who does not walk in step with the wicked or stand in the way that sinners take or sit in the company of mockers, but whose delight is in the law of the Lord, and who meditates on his law day and night. That person is like a tree planted by streams of water, which yields its fruit in season and whose leaf does not wither—whatever they do prospers (1:1-3, NIV).

When you sit with God's Word, how do you feel? Angry? Bitter? Drained? In pain?

Or do you feel peace? Calm? Mercy? Love? Acceptance?

Let me ask you this. What else do you seek to truly fulfil and nurture your soul? What if the most beautiful moments in life are tucked away into this time with God that will ultimately satisfy our deepest longings? This sounds so wonderful, yet I still find myself at times grasping instead for the fleeting things that barely even satisfy. I reach for things that do not feed my soul with goodness the way that Jesus does.

Are you planting yourself by streams of water or in the desert?

When you meditate on the Word of God, you are planting yourself by streams of water. The tree that does that will yield its fruit. If you are not feeling fruitful, is it perhaps because you are planted on parched land? We can't get sustenance where there is none.

It's been many years since that moment in my kitchen feeling like I was in a powerless to stop freefalling. But when I chose to soak in the Word of God, I absolutely felt held up. Because the truth is that the love and comfort of Jesus in those dark, hard, out-of-control moments when we let him in and let him transform us in our deepest hurt become the most powerful and beautiful moments of victory in our lives. That time, although horrible, now feels like one of the most redeeming moments of my walk with God when I look back on it. He provided for me what I needed in that season, and every season. When I couldn't hold on, I had to plant myself instead.

So, I close my eyes and instead of feeling the freefall, my feet feel firmly planted. I hear a stream, a river bringing life and abundance to me. I sense peace that surpasses understanding (Philippians 4:7) and feel my heart bursting from the beauty returned to me from the ashes (Isaiah 61:3). These moments feel like heaven on Earth. A glimpse into eternity through the pain. My heart's desires fulfilled. Joy. Knowing these moments with Jesus, no matter the season, are some of the most beautiful pleasures in this world.

Declaration

Delight yourself in the LORD, and he will give you the desires of your heart (Psalm 37:4, ESV).

Questions

How do you feel after you have spent time with Jesus during the day?

What specific sustenance from God do you need right now? Consider the fruits of the spirit (love, joy, peace, patience, kindness, goodness, faithfulness, gentleness, and self-control)?

Prayer

Write a prayer to God asking for Him to give you growth in the area(s) you indicated in the question above.

Day 24:
Correct Footwear

When my husband and I first started dating, we took a winter hike to see a waterfall near his parents' house. When we walked down the path back to our car after seeing the waterfall, I noticed some very odd-looking footprints in the snow. They appeared to be high-heeled shoe prints.

"What kind of a person wears shoes like that to a place like this?" I asked.

It was slippery enough in the Puma runners I was wearing. How could anyone be wearing high heels here? When we got closer to the parking lot, my husband looked down and noticed something. The footprints that I had been judging were actually mine!

They may not have been the high heels I thought were trudging through the snow, but they were not proper shoes for our journey either.

It became a joke in our relationship that I never wear the right footwear, but they say behind every joke is some truth. We had been married for five years before I finally bought proper winter boots.

God's Word can be like equipping ourselves with the proper footwear to walk through life.

As we walk through different seasons in our lives, we will need the appropriate protection on our feet for the terrain, temperature, and distance. I don't wear flip flops in the winter because my feet would be frozen. I don't hike a mountain in high heels either. But there are warm summer days when we should wear flip flops to protect our feet from the hot sand at the beach, and spring days when we need rainboots to keep our feet dry. God's Word in our hearts will be like equipping our feet with the appropriate footwear. They protect our hearts from the elements we may face.

Proper footwear does not change the season, but it allows us to endure it.

Another incident happened with those same Puma shoes a year later.

My husband and I did a 16-kilometre hike around a mountain lake. My Pumas had thin soles and left my feet so sore from stepping on sharp rocks and roots sticking up out of the ground that by our last kilometre I was limping along in absolute agony. I was only 26 and in relatively good shape, but my improper footwear was my absolute undoing. As I struggled along, two ladies in their sixties wearing sturdy hiking boots came up behind us.

"Excuse us!" they said, and they walked past briskly, without any pain holding them back.

I felt extremely pathetic. Those ladies were hiking the same trail and there I was, nearly in tears from my sore feet.

I finally got to the parking lot and took off the shoes to walk across the pavement to the car. I figured that nothing could hurt more than wearing those shoes any further. And I was right. Bare feet on asphalt felt amazing compared to another second in those shoes.

"What kind of person wears shoes like that to a place like this?" my husband jokingly asked, referring back to our waterfall hike.

It's true. It wasn't the trail's fault that I didn't dress properly.

We are not guaranteed a smooth life. It's WHEN we face trials, not IF we face them. It's up to me to put on the correct footwear. It would be absurd to expect a nice smooth paved trail around a mountain lake. The beauty of the hike was in the rocky trail.

His Word is enough to equip you to walk the journey he has ahead of you. He has made this promise to you.

Reading and immersing ourselves in the Word of God and spending time in prayer is like being prepared and buying the right shoes for all the right situations.

> If you say, "The Lord is my refuge," and you make the Most High your dwelling, no harm will overtake you, no disaster will come near your tent. For he will command his angels concerning you to guard you in all your ways; they will lift you up in their hands, so that you will not strike your foot against a stone. You will tread on the lion and the cobra; you will trample the great lion and the serpent (Psalm 91:9-13, NIV).

May we prepare for our spiritual walk the same way we should plan for hikes or a rainy day walk.

I regret waiting five years to buy proper winter boots. But now that I have, there have been countless beautiful winter hikes with warm feet and no pain at all. The time is now. Get your closet ready.

Declaration

Stand firm then, with the belt of truth buckled around your waist, with the breastplate of righteousness in place, and with your feet fitted with the readiness that comes from the gospel of peace (Ephesians 6:14-15, NIV).

Questions

Was there a time in your life where you went through a difficult situation and felt like God had prepared you in advance? A situation where God had shown his protection and provision over you?

Have you gone through a difficult time when you did not feel like you were spiritually ready?

How would you describe the difference in your spiritual response in both cases?

Prayer

Write a prayer to God thanking him for the ways that your spiritual life and prayers have already got you through difficult times. Ask him to show you the areas that you need to grow in readiness.

Day 25: Highway Hypnosis

When driving, it is a common phenomenon that when we arrive at our destination (think about arriving home after work) we do not remember any details of the drive or how we got there. We sometimes say we were "on autopilot". This phenomenon is quite real and actually has a name: highway hypnosis (Naoumidis, 2020). In this state we still respond and process our surroundings and respond in ways that allow us to drive safely. It is a little terrifying to think we weren't really fully present, but we have all had it happen to us enough that we trust the process when it happens. We arrive home we aren't really sure how we got there.

When I first began driving a car, I was very scared that I would side swipe someone on my passenger side. It seemed unnatural to have so much car on that side of me. After a lot of practice and driving experience, I now never need to think about where the side of the car is. My spatial awareness of the edges of the vehicle are ingrained in my subconscious.

With enough practice, driving a car becomes a natural thing to do. We don't have to think about every little detail. We can get to our destination without even thinking about it or being fully in the moment. Driving flows much more seamlessly the more we do it, and eventually we can do it without thinking about it at all. We are driving around with highway hypnosis, and nobody is in danger.

In my spiritual life, there are so many areas God has chosen to grow within my heart that have felt very unnatural, like driving a car for the first few times. Spiritual growth can be awkward and feel strange. It can be something that we need to constantly think about and focus our energy on.

For example, forgiveness. This was something I was not taught to extend as a child. I was taught to hold grudges, because my mom held grudges against me. I hadn't received forgiveness from my mom for my mistakes as a child. How could I extend forgiveness to others? It felt like someone threw me into a full-size truck and forced me onto the freeway with no driving experience. I had no idea how to steer, change lanes, or merge, and all of it felt like I was in danger and going to die. Nothing about forgiveness came naturally to me. I didn't know where I was going. Nothing about those first few journeys felt anything like highway hypnosis.

Building spiritual disciplines will feel a lot like driving a car for the first time. You have to think about every tiny detail. It is so much easier to go back to what feels normal or easy. However, we do not choose to walk forever just because driving feels awkward at first. Instead, we keep practicing because we know driving a vehicle is a worthwhile skill for life. Having your driver's license is a whole new level of freedom. So is a close relationship with Jesus.

Some days, pulling out your Bible will feel like a waste of your time. You have a long to-do list, and your Bible seems like the easiest thing to put off until later. It's clunky and awkward moving a very real to-do list to the side for time in scripture, because a check mark for reading scripture might not feel like we actually did anything worthwhile.

This is how it feels at first. But when you keep at it day after day, it becomes as natural to grab your Bible and sit down with it for a few minutes as it does to grab your phone and sit down to scroll for a few minutes.

Perhaps sitting down in your special spot with your Bible and your coffee becomes a phenomenon like highway hypnosis. Can we call it Bible hypnosis? Without realizing how you got there, you are curled up with your Bible on your favourite chair with your favourite drink. I'm sure it took months of driving practice and lessons before you ever experienced highway hypnosis. And it may take a while before you find you settle into your Bible hypnosis pattern too.

We often believe the lie that we aren't disciplined enough to get into a routine. "That is for other people," we reason. But we ARE able to get into routines. We ARE able to reach for the Bible on autopilot as if it's second nature. In the same way we safely navigate our way to our homes, we will safely navigate our way to Jesus.

In Ephesians 3:16-19, Paul shares his prayer for the church in Ephesus:

> I pray that from his glorious, unlimited resources he will empower you with inner strength through his Spirit. Then Christ will make his home in your hearts as you trust in him. Your roots will grow down into God's love and keep you strong. And may you have the power to understand, as all God's people should, how wide, how long, how high, and how deep his love is. May you experience the love of Christ, though it is too great to understand fully. Then you will be made complete with all the fullness of life and power that comes from God (NLT).

Let me just repeat that last part for you.

"You will be made complete with all the fullness of life and power that comes from God."

This is a prayer that I pray for you too. That as you learn this new rhythm of living that you will find so much more for the nourishment of your soul than you can find at the bottom of a completed to-do list. That these moments with Jesus give you fullness, power, and a deep-rooted understanding of Christ's love for you. You will not be made complete by getting it all done first, then engaging with Jesus.

You will not be made complete by making excuses.

You will be made complete when he empowers you. When he strengthens you because you allow him to make his home in your heart. Where you connect so automatically you just end up in his embrace without even having to think about it.

Declaration

And in Christ you have been brought to fullness. He is the head over every power and authority (Colossians 2:10, NIV).

Questions

What things in life do you often do without even thinking?

Is there something you do without thinking that is destructive in some way? How is it destructive? Would you like to stop? Take a moment to acknowledge that you have got into a bad habit and think about how you could change.

Prayer

Write a prayer asking God to help you replace a bad habit with a good habit.

Day 26:
Reap What You Sow

I am not much of a gardening person, but I do plant a garden every spring. For many years, I have planted things that I never end up using. I don't really use the mint I plant. I can't possibly eat 100 carrots that are ready the same week. And I am not sure why I even plant tomatoes! They usually end up with a mealy texture, and I am probably not planting the ones that are right for my climate zone.

Regardless of how well my garden thrives, if I end up using it, or if my produce tastes okay, there is one thing about it that is successful every year: the type of seeds I plant grow into the type of plant shown on the package. I'm not planting lettuce and getting corn.

We know this is true for gardening. But we take this less seriously when it comes to the seeds we sow in our lives.

Sowing can mean to plant or scatter seeds. But sowing is also defined as "setting in motion" (Merriam-Webster, 2024).

For example, if we set in motion a physical fitness plan, we will reap a harvest of strength, endurance, and health.

But there are other more subtle seeds we plant in our lives.

We plant things in our minds that will reap a harvest too. And just like my garden in the spring, I choose what I plant in my mental garden. I am really trying my best to plant only the things that I know will be useful to me. I don't want to keep planting things that just take up space but are not needed.

> Don't be misled—you cannot mock the justice of God. You will always harvest what you plant. Those who live only to satisfy their own sinful nature will harvest decay and death from that sinful nature. But those who live to please the Spirit will harvest everlasting life from the Spirit. So let's not get

> tired of doing what is good. At just the right time we will reap a harvest of blessing if we don't give up (Galatians 6:7-9, NLT).

If we scatter the seeds of endless scrolling on social media, we will reap a harvest of insecurity and wasted time. If displaying our own life on social media for others to scroll through is what we focus our thoughts on endlessly, we will reap a harvest of needing the approval of others.

If we plant seeds of popular opinion, we will reap a harvest that doesn't always mirror Jesus' views.

If we plant toxic people in our lives, we will end up with toxic relationships that drain us.

If we sow fear in our lives, we will reap a harvest of that same fear.

An honest look at our lives and how we spend our time and energy can reveal the seeds that we are planting. Even the smallest of seeds can grow into the biggest tree in the garden.

"He told them another parable: 'The kingdom of heaven is like a mustard seed, which a man took and planted in his field. Though it is the smallest of all seeds, yet when it grows, it is the largest of garden plants and becomes a tree, so that the birds come and perch in its branches'" (Matthew 13:31-32, NIV).

It is not the size of the seed that matters, but the type.

If we plant seeds of scripture in our heart day after day, we will grow a garden full of the knowledge of God.

When we plant truth in our life day after day, we will harvest confidence and steadfastness.

If we plant wisdom in our life day after day, we will harvest discernment.

After my kids and I plant all our seeds in the garden we must wait for a few days or weeks before we see the seeds sprout. In the same way, when we start these new routines we do not necessarily see the results growing right away. It might feel like the effort is for nothing and we aren't feeling better, more spiritual, or more peaceful. In the garden, we eventually see a little sprout, and it doesn't look like we expect it to. We wonder, "Is that really a carrot poking out of the ground, or is that just a weed?" Those first few weeks of growth don't look like much, and they certainly do not look like the final product.

Just keep watering those righteous seeds you plant in hopes of a fully flourishing garden. Growth takes time. But if you planted the right seeds, you will see the right crops.

Declaration

"The Lord will indeed give what is good, and our land will yield its harvest" (Psalm 85:12, NIV).

Questions

Have you taken steps to purposefully plant good seeds? What were they? What did you reap from planting even the smallest seeds?

What seeds do you need to plant in your life going forward? What do you want to grow in your garden? Do you have spiritual goals for the future? How can you take one tiny step and plant that seed, starting today?

Prayer

Write a prayer to God asking him to show you which seeds you need to start planting in your life. You may not know what you will need as a crop for your future, but God does. Ask him to show you.

Day 27:
Jesus' Feet

If I am being honest about the way I have lived my life, I should tell you that I have spent a lot of time grovelling in the dust. It may not be a literal roll in the dust. But I get down low and beg the world for scraps of approval or affirmation. I beat myself up with thoughts that question my own worth. Fear sometimes leaves me in the fetal position where I am too afraid to rise up and embrace my identity in Christ. When I am not in my risen position with Christ holding my identity, I am down in the dust with someone else.

At the fall in the Garden of Eden, the first thing the Lord said to the serpent was, "Because you have done this, you are cursed more than all animals, domestic and wild. You will crawl on your belly, groveling in the dust as long as you live" (Genesis 3:14, NLT).

Some days I spend more of my time in the dust like the serpent, punishing myself for something that God has redeemed me from, than I do walking in the freedom Christ has given me. The serpent wants us to think that we are in the dust with him. He wants us grovelling at the feet of the world hoping for some sort of meaning or acceptance or looking to the world to give us peace and fulfillment.

If you are laying in the dust, I want to remind you that is also where you will find the feet of Jesus.

Life takes a drastic turn at the feet of Jesus. The final nail for your redemption was driven into his feet.

During his time on Earth and even in his resurrection, Jesus' feet were the place where he was willing to meet us. Being present at his feet is actually what he said was the one thing that we should be concerning ourselves with.

In the story of Martha and Mary in Luke 10:38-42, Mary sat at the feet of Jesus:

> As Jesus and the disciples continued on their way to Jerusalem, they came to a certain village where a woman named Martha welcomed him into her home. Her sister, Mary, sat at the Lord's feet, listening to what he taught. But Martha was distracted by the big dinner she was preparing. She came to Jesus and said, "Lord, doesn't it seem unfair to you that my sister just sits here while I do all the work? Tell her to come and help me." But the Lord said to her, "My dear Martha, you are worried and upset over all these details! There is only one thing worth being concerned about. Mary has discovered it, and it will not be taken away from her" (NLT).

Life gets hectic and we all have a long to-do list, just like Martha. The demands never stop. But sitting at his feet is the one thing Jesus needs us to be concerned with. The distractions of looking for worth, approval, or security or completing our daily tasks are not a worthy excuse to stay away. Jesus commands us to stop with the worry and stress and sit at his feet.

Another woman who we read about in Luke 7:36-50 also had an encounter at the feet of Jesus. The Bible refers to her as "The Sinful Woman". I really hope that if the most-read book in all of history was to reference me, it would find a better way to name me than "The Sinful Woman"! But this particular woman was also very brave. In fact, I envy her bravery. I personally would rather not draw attention to my sinfulness. We all tend to perfectly curate the person people see on social media or in person. But this woman went into someone else's home, broke tradition, and did not care what the other people in the room thought of her, even though they scoffed at her actions. She then anointed the feet of Jesus.

What would motivate her to anoint his feet with perfume in spite of all that she had done? This woman knew she was forgiven. Jesus told her she was forgiven. Her act towards Jesus at his feet was out of gratitude for what he had already done, not grovelling. At the feet of Jesus, she was "The Forgiven Woman".

Even John the Baptist introduces Jesus into the world by referencing the holiness of his feet:

> The people were waiting expectantly and were all wondering in their hearts if John might possibly be the Messiah. John answered them all, "I baptize you with water. But one who is more powerful than I will come, the straps of whose sandals I am not worthy to untie. He will baptize you with the Holy Spirit and fire" (Luke 3:15-16, NIV).

Jesus carried out his preaching ministry by walking and spreading his message. And even after defeating death, his feet led him to walk alongside his disciples on the road to Emmaus (Luke 24:15).

As I sit in these revelations about the feet of Jesus, I am humbled. Although the serpent wants to take me down to his level, laying in the dust, crawling along on my belly, I am able to bring my whole self to the feet of Jesus. Jesus himself declared this is what we need most. At the feet of Jesus, he disciples us. His feet are a resting place in a world of busy schedules and demands. His feet are a place of forgiveness. Through his feet, he took the punishment for our sin and carried the weight of it. But it is also through his feet that we are introduced to his sovereignty and righteousness. His feet took his resurrected body back to his closest friends, and he is still walking alongside us today.

And we in turn get to be the ones to carry on his message as we walk through life.

"How beautiful on the mountains are the feet of the messenger who brings good news, the good news of peace and salvation, the news that the God of Israel reigns" (Isaiah 52:7, NLT)!

Declaration

For you have delivered me from death and my feet from stumbling, that I may walk before God in the light of life (Psalm 56:13, NIV).

Questions

In what areas of your life do you feel like you are grovelling in the dust with the serpent?

Do you feel like you are able to encounter Jesus when you feel like you are grovelling in the dust? Do you feel like he is kneeling down beside you?

Prayer

Imagine you are sitting at the feet of Jesus right now. What would you ask him or say to him? Write it out as a prayer.

Day 28:
Two Truths and a Lie

Small groups for building community have long been a passion of mine and I have been fortunate enough to lead quite a few of them. When leading groups with young adults, one of my favourite ice breakers on our first night together is a game called "Two Truths and a Lie".

In this game, everyone writes three statements about themselves. Two of the statements are true and one of them is a lie. The group will then take a moment to think and look the person they don't know up and down, trying to figure them out. Then, each person will have a chance to guess which of the three statements is a lie.

Every once in a while, I would be in a group of people where I already knew something about a few of the members. They weren't complete strangers. For these people, I would have an advantage and a better shot at guessing correctly which of their statements was a lie.

"I have a twin," a casual acquaintance would say. I'd feel confident I would have known this by now if it was true, so I could deduce that "I have a twin" must be the lie.

There would also be groups where I would have a close friend there with me. In that case, there really wouldn't be any way to fool me. I would always be able to sniff out the lie because I knew that person really well.

I could determine what the lie was, because I knew the truth about who that person was.

As I go about my days, there are random moments where thoughts pop into my head. Thoughts that when I type them out, they sound so far from true. But when I hear them in my head, they feel so very true indeed.

"You aren't good enough."

"You are too much for them."

"You are ugly."

"You will fail if you try that."

"You should be afraid right now!"

However, the more I know Jesus and the closer we become in relationship, the more I am able to identify the lies of the enemy that come at me.

Just because we hear a lie in our mind does not make it true. I may feel a certain way, but feelings are not facts. Things I can feel in my heart are not from Jesus.

Jeremiah 17:9 says, "The human heart is the most deceitful of all things, and desperately wicked. Who really knows how bad it is?" (NLT)

I am sure I know where those thoughts originate. I have an enemy that is after my heart. The trouble is, I can hear God in my heart, but I can also hear the enemy in my heart.

So, who am I to listen to? Well, I know that I need to listen to God, but I have to be able to know his voice when I hear it.

Like in the game of "Two Truths and a Lie", the better I know someone the easier it is to sniff out the lie.

The same is true for our relationship with God. The more intimately I know Him, His voice, and His truth, the easier it will be when the lies of the enemy enter my heart. Not only can I detect the lie, but I can also identify the truth.

"We demolish arguments and every pretension that sets itself up against the knowledge of God, and we take captive every thought to make it obedient to Christ" (2 Corinthians 10:5, NIV).

I knew some people in my small groups very well because I spent time with them. I had listened to their story, hopes, and dreams and connected deeply with them. When we know someone well, we know if what we are hearing rings true or not.

It's agonizing to live with these lies consuming us day in and day out. I don't know anyone who enjoys feeling brought down by the lies of the enemy. On the contrary, I am brought to life when I hear stories of people who overcame the lies of the enemy and lived out the truth.

It starts by knowing God intimately. Knowing his voice. His character. This knowledge comes from speaking to him in prayer and silently listening to him respond. Tuning out the noise and distractions.

It does take time and energy to get to know God more and more deeply. But the result is a more peaceful life. A life where you can filter out the lies and in turn make your thoughts obedient to Christ.

It's a solid return on investment of your time when you are no longer captive to the lies of the enemy.

Declaration

I have been crucified with Christ and I no longer live, but Christ lives in me (Galatians 2:20a, NIV).

Questions

List two truths that you know about God, his character, his love for you, and his providence over your life. List one lie that you find yourself getting trapped in.

Prayer

Ask God to show you his truth in contrast with the lie that you wrote down. Write this truth down below.

Day 29:
Once is Never Enough

One of the best feelings in the world is when you walk out of your very last final exam of the semester and know that you are free.

I have walked out of many final exams thinking, "Yikes, I didn't know any of that." And, I have walked out of exams feeling like I knew almost everything. But one thing that is similar between these experiences is that regardless of how much I know, I forget a lot of it the moment I walk out of the classroom door.

While I hope this isn't completely true for a lot of people we trust with our lives (think doctors and nurses), when you walk away from studying daily you are going to lose some (or in my case, a lot) of that information, especially if it ends up being the last time you ever immerse yourself in that subject.

After we finish school and begin our careers, we often take part in ongoing education or professional development activities to stay current with innovation in our field and to make sure we retain necessary knowledge. The day of our last final exam will not be the last time we need what we learned in school if we want to be successful in a related career.

A life with Jesus as the Lord and leader of our lives is not a one and done experience either. We know him best when we are continually in the Word, not unlike the continuing education we do for our careers.

In John 8:12, Jesus said, "I am the light of the world. Whoever follows me will never walk in darkness, but will have the light of life" (NIV).

He is clear that we need to follow him to have that light. By following him, he is asking us to stay current with him. Following is not a one and done event. It is continuous and ongoing.

I have friends who speak a tremendous amount of truth into my life. They are encouraging and fun, and they rejuvenate me. For that relationship to develop, it would not have been enough to meet them once. I didn't introduce myself and then walk away from them and that was it. I love to hear their voice, their wisdom, and their encouragement constantly. I need them to pour into me regularly. I need that connection and those reminders as I navigate through life that I am loved, thought of, and cared for. I need my friends to stay with me in life.

It's not one and done with the people in our lives who we love, and neither is our walk through scripture.

Although scripture never changes, it is alive and active (Hebrews 4:12). We need it to accompany us as we journey through this life just like we need our friends to walk out life beside us. Scripture is not just knowledge to be read or studied once. It is alive to help us navigate us through life, speaking into our lives just like our beloved friends and family who care deeply for us.

I don't want a doctor who memorized a medical textbook 30 years ago and then stopped studying medicine. I don't want to jump from new acquaintance to new acquaintance, never going deeper and never building a true friendship. And I certainly don't want to read the Word of God once and then struggle to have a deep relationship with Jesus.

There is no final exam, but there is a final destination. Do we know where we are going and who we are moving towards? We will if we walk with him and stay in his light and connected to his love continually. Once is never enough.

Declaration

The unfolding of your words gives light; it gives understanding to the simple (Psalm 119:130, NIV).

Questions

Pick one chapter in the Bible that had a lot of meaning in a previous season of life. Read it twice. Is there something new that stood out to you today that has never stood out before?

Prayer

Write a prayer asking God to reveal to you new revelations through his Word as you read your Bible more. Is there anything in this season of life that you would like God to show you wisdom in? Ask him in your prayer.

Day 30:
Don't Ask Me to Bake You a Cake

I have a confession, now that we've been on this devotional journey together for a while now. It's not a popular opinion to have. But I will own it nonetheless.

I do not like baking.

I know a lot of people find joy and peace in baking. That is not true for me. I don't enjoy measuring things. I don't like reading recipes. I like to make things I don't have to think too much about. I also do not like washing dishes. Huge mixing bowls, cake pans, and other items that won't fit in my dishwasher or are not dishwasher safe are not fun to wash and dry and put away. It all just seems like too much effort.

When I need to mix things together in a special order, I admit that I don't. I throw it all in and hope for the best. To be honest, this method works pretty well for me. I haven't had too many things flop. My baking is haphazard at best because I am usually just trying to get it over with.

Once in my rush to bake a cake, I didn't even set the timer, because I was eager to get my dishes out of the way. Realizing my mistake, I pulled the cake out to check and try to estimate how much time was left. Unfortunately, pulling it out far too early caused the cake to go flat in the middle.

It tasted okay to me, and since I didn't have a food critic coming over to try the cake (my kids, although food critics, do not count in this case), it would pass. Nobody in my family complained that the chocolate cake wasn't quite right in the middle.

The same can be said about our faith. We are on a journey to become more Christ-like. I would love for that to happen quickly and without any trials that are going to grow my faith. Unfortunately, Jesus doesn't work with quick fixes. Like a cake in the oven, we can't rush the process. We can't switch out the proper ingredients and expect it to work. I can't remove the baking powder or the sugar and expect a cake to actually work, or to be worth eating. And I cannot move a cake early in the baking process or it will fall flat in the middle.

James 1:2-4 says,

> Consider it a sheer gift, friends, when tests and challenges come at you from all sides. You know that under pressure, your faith-life is forced into the open and shows its true colors. So don't try to get out of anything prematurely. Let it do its work so you become mature and well-developed, not deficient in any way (MSG).

You can't get out of this journey prematurely. You are not alone. Stay the course. Consider it a sheer gift that you are here right now. You aren't at the beginning, and you aren't at the end. This is the gift of right now, where God is growing you faithfully. Your spiritual maturity, like a cake baking in the oven, is not a cake until it is done baking. If you pull it out too early, you risk damaging the final result. You have to just allow the process of growth to happen as God has planned it out in advance. Like the anticipation of a cake baking and the lovely aroma of what is to come, there are small signs of growth that you can learn to find satisfying.

You might read your Bible for days at a time, and maybe it doesn't feel like God is doing anything in your life. You might not feel like it is making a difference. Your trials are still your trials. Your fears are still your fears.

Do not lose heart in this process. Your cake is inedible the whole time it is baking. But that doesn't mean that it will not be a cake in the end, if we allow it to bake. Some things are not done until they are done. Be grateful for the days that Jesus has given you. He loves you too much to leave you where you are. He is working on you when you do not see it. Do not give up hope.

"Being confident of this, that he who began a good work in you will carry it on to completion until the day of Christ Jesus" (Philippians 1:6, NIV).

All of the stages of growth are important to him, and he has not forsaken you. He will finish what he has started. And he didn't put the ingredients together in the wrong order like I do. He didn't miss an ingredient either. He knows exactly what he is doing to grow you into the most beautiful reflection of his glory. I may not like baking cakes, but God is certainly in the business of putting things together just right.

Declaration

For we are God's handiwork, created in Christ Jesus to do good works, which God prepared in advance for us to do (Ephesians 2:20, NIV).

Questions

Is there an area in your life that you feel frustrated God hasn't redeemed or changed?

What are some small ways that you see God working in that situation?

Prayer

Write a prayer asking God to continue to work in that area of your life. Bring your need to him. Don't sugarcoat it! He can handle your fear, doubt, or discouragement.

Day 31:
Renewing your Mind

By the time my 11th anniversary rolled around, my husband and I had an inside joke, just between us. He alleged that I had changed so much that he was now married to an entirely different person than the one he exchanged wedding vows with on our wedding day.

I am sure that over the course of a lifetime this rings true for a lot of people. We all naturally change and evolve. We may become mothers, or change careers, or find and pursue different interests, move, or live a different lifestyle.

In my case, I grew up in a house where my interests and opinions were heavily criticized. If what I felt or liked didn't align with what my family liked or believed, it was shot down. So, I learned to go with the status quo to keep the peace. Whenever I had a different opinion, I quickly realized it was best to stick with the shared opinion of everyone else. I never felt comfortable expanding my vision because it was more trouble than it was worth.

But when I got married and started my own family, all of that began to change.

I realized that I am a huge fan of classic rock music. I don't like country music as much as I thought I did.

I came from a non-Christian household. Although I was a Christian when I got married, there were still more changes that happened within me when I stopped looking to the acceptable opinion to keep the peace. I could now read what the Bible said and I realized I had the freedom to think, say, and speak what I felt about it. I could do more than just read it. I felt safe and comfortable to let the words saturate my spirit, challenge my previously accepted beliefs, and transform my mind.

In Romans 12:2 Paul writes to us, "Don't copy the behaviour and customs of this world, but let God transform you into a new person by changing the way you think. Then you will learn to know God's will for you, which is good and pleasing and perfect" (NLT).

I had no idea when I began my journey of daily Bible reading that the popular or safe opinions I had taken on as my own were going to be transformed. Be open to finding yourself change when you start reading your Bible and praying daily!

God changed my heart towards things I never expected. It was exciting and refreshing! Sometimes, it is terrifying to think about how far off biblical truth my truth had become. The longer I have spent in the Word, the more I have realized that what I thought lined up with scripture actually lined up more with culture than biblical truth.

The only way we can have these realizations is to continually renew our minds in the Word. It isn't something we do once and become set for life. We are constantly growing towards maturity.

> Then we will no longer be infants, tossed back and forth by the waves, and blown here and there by every wind of teaching and by the cunning and craftiness of people in their deceitful scheming. Instead, speaking the truth in love, we will grow to become in every respect the mature body of him who is the head, that is, Christ (Ephesians 4:14-15, NIV).

We will be anchored in the Word of God, and we will grow to maturity.

The views, opinions, and perspectives of the world will not be the loudest voices in our lives. It won't matter what the people around us say or think. We won't feel like we need to conform to peoples' expectations of our opinions. We will conform to the Word of God.

Even within the church, there are people we may encounter who do not know scripture because they actually have not taken the time to read through the Bible. It is important to have our own first-hand knowledge of what the Bible says, as well as having wise teachers walk alongside us guiding our understanding. We can all think of times that scripture has been misused, taken out of context, or used incorrectly to push a certain agenda.

But when we know first-hand what the Bible says, we do not fall into that trap. We do not get pushed around by lies. We are free to read the Bible and be wholly and 100% open to truth. Then we can live that truth. The Bible tells us that this truth sets us free. And I can tell you from my own experience that this is true.

"So, Jesus said to the Jews who had believed him, 'If you abide in my word, you are truly my disciples, and you will know the truth, and the truth will set you free'" (John 8:31-32, ESV).

As for my marriage, my husband actually prefers having a wife that has embraced the truth of God, even when it meant changing so much about herself. He loves the changes. (Especially the part where I do not listen to country music anymore.)

Declaration

Therefore we do not lose heart. Though outwardly we are wasting away, yet inwardly we are being renewed day by day (2 Corinthians 4:16, NIV).

Questions

Has scripture ever changed your view on an area in your life? Did you fight the change or embrace it?

Have you ever misinterpreted a scripture verse out of context? What was the verse and how did you misunderstand it? What is the truth you know now?

Prayer

Write a prayer asking God to open your heart to truth. Ask him to show you his truth unclouded by preconceived ideas, cultural influences, or anything else that may block your ability to take truth in clearly.

Day 32:
Fake Fruit Trees

A friend of mine built a home in a new neighbourhood that was named after a type of fruit garden. At the entrance to this neighbourhood were fake trees. Three big metal apple trees greeted you as you drove along the main street. It felt like quite the juxtaposition, having metal trees welcome you to this supposed garden.

There was no actual fruit to be found.

> You can identify them by their fruit, that is, by the way they act. Can you pick grapes from thornbushes, or figs from thistles? A good tree produces good fruit, and a bad tree produces bad fruit. A good tree can't produce bad fruit, and a bad tree can't produce good fruit. So every tree that does not produce good fruit is chopped down and thrown into the fire. Yes, just as you can identify a tree by its fruit, so you can identify people by their actions (Matthew 7:16-20, NLT).

Just as this neighbourhood faked being full of fruit, we can often fake the true state of our heart. But what is inside of us will determine what we produce. Do our lives showcase the fruits of the spirit? Can people see love, joy, peace, forbearance, kindness, goodness, faithfulness, gentleness and self-control in our lives (Galatians 5:22-23)?

We might think we are doing okay if the people around us believe that we are doing okay. They can't see our heart, so if we appear to be fruitful, maybe that's alright. The truth is, we know if the trees that we have on display are metal and just for show or if they are real trees producing real fruit in our lives.

Do you know what happens to these metal fruit trees after a few years? The sun bleaches the paint on them. The paint gets chipped. Then rust starts eating them away. And as the years pass, there is no fruit to show. Year after year, these trees never produce a single crop.

In contrast, think about what happens to real fruit trees. They grow bigger and fuller. They produce fruit in season. Real trees also require watering and maintenance such as pruning. They require someone to pick the fruit.

So, the end result is either rust or sustenance.

We may have been surviving on faux faith in the past. But that does not mean that we need to continue to live that way. We can pretend we are satisfied with a fake alternative, or we can strive to grow a real garden of abundance.

Have we erected fake trees because they take no effort to maintain, but then realize they also produce no fruit?

When I commented to my friend who lived in this supposed "orchard" that the fake metal trees seemed a bit silly to me when the neighbourhood could have planted real trees just as (or more) easily, she said, "I actually really like the look of the fake trees better!"

Ok. Wow.

Some people will prefer the look of the fake trees in your life. There will be people around you who will be satisfied with you not growing a real, authentic, thriving relationship with Jesus. Why? Because they aren't growing either.

Fake trees look less foolish if they are next to other fake trees. If these metal tree ornaments were situated in a real orchard full of real, strong, healthy trees, they would look absurd. Now, no disrespect to my friend. Our conversation was not about faith, and maybe we just have a different artistic eye. But the reality is that when it comes to fake versus real spiritual fruit, not everyone will be cheering you on along your journey to true fruitfulness.

We can be satisfied with a fake alternative, or we can strive to grow a garden of real abundance.

The Bible has many descriptions of real trees and real growth:

"The land produced vegetation: plants bearing seed according to their kinds and trees bearing fruit with seed in it according to their kinds. And God saw that it was good" (Genesis 1:12, NIV).

"The righteous will flourish like a palm tree, they will grow like a cedar of Lebanon" (Psalm 92:12, NIV).

"He told them another parable: 'The kingdom of heaven is like a mustard seed, which a man took and planted in his field. Though it is the smallest of all seeds, yet when it grows, it is the largest of garden plants and becomes a tree, so that the birds come and perch in its branches'" (Matthew 13:31-32, NIV).

"Still other seed fell on good soil, where it produced a crop—a hundred, sixty or thirty times what was sown" (Matthew 13:8, NIV).

"He will also send you rain for the seed you sow in the ground, and the food that comes from the land will be rich and plentiful. In that day your cattle will graze in broad meadows" (Isaiah 32:23, NIV).

"Wisdom is a tree of life to those who embrace her; happy are those who hold her tightly" (Proverbs 3:18, NLT).

"But blessed is the one who trusts in the Lord, whose confidence is in him. They will be like a tree planted by the water that sends out its roots by the stream. It does not fear when heat comes; its leaves are always green. It has no worries in a year of drought and never fails to bear fruit." (Jeremiah 17:8, NIV).

But to see fruit in your life, you must get up and begin to tend to your orchard. Plant real seeds into real soil. Pull the weeds. Fertilize. Give your trees a deep root water. Give them light and prune away the dead parts. A tree can take a whole lifetime to grow. Little by little, bit by bit.

Our faith journey may seem like that at times. But in due time, if we put in the gardening work and do not give up, we will see the fruit.

Declaration

He cuts off every branch in me that bears no fruit, while every branch that does bear fruit he prunes so that it will be even more fruitful (John 15:2, NIV).

Questions

Consider the fruits of the Spirit listed in Galatians 5:22-23: love, joy, peace, forbearance, kindness, goodness, faithfulness, gentleness and self-control. Which of these fruits do you see in your life? Are there additional areas of fruitfulness and growth in your life right now?

What fruits would you like to see in your life right now? In what areas do you feel called to increase your fruitfulness? (You can refer to the fruits of the Spirit.) Is there an area where you would like to see more growth? (e.g., your marriage, your family, relationships with others, with God, with your church, your community)

Prayer

Write a prayer asking Jesus to show you the next steps to take in your faith journey to grow the spiritual fruits you listed above or the other areas of growth that you are feeling called towards.

Day 33: Bread Alone

I had just finished feeling better after being sick when my throat started to feel scratchy again. It ended up being a long two weeks of back-to-back illnesses and my energy levels were low, but I wanted to do what I could to make myself feel better as soon as possible.

Plenty of liquids, rest, and a good diet were what would help with that.

When I was hungry, it felt all too easy to grab quick junk food. It is much faster and easier to microwave something less than healthy to eat when my energy levels were so low. Or, it would have been so satisfying to just grab takeout from a drive-through rather than take the extra few minutes to make a kale smoothie or a salad.

I would wonder then if I should just have a cup of coffee or try to take a nap.

Relieving hunger with empty calories is not the same as eating a healthy diet. In the moment, they may both alleviate hunger pangs. But they do not fuel your body the same way.

Either proper sleep or coffee could get you through your day. But only one of them will actually provide healing, rest, and rejuvenation.

There are many ways we try to sustain ourselves other than food. We feed ourselves with social media, seeking approval of others, success, materialism, and entertainment.

Just like microwaving a burrito or ordering another round of fast food, we live off what we consume mentally, whether it ends up being good for us in the long run or not.

I would eventually recover from my sickness if I ate a diet of junk. But that doesn't mean that I have taken care of myself in the best possible way.

The enemy wants us to settle for feeling full on a diet of emptiness.

The enemy wants us to come to him and not God to feel satisfied. But this isn't real lasting satisfaction or health.

When Jesus was led into the wilderness to be tested, the devil said to him, "If you are the Son of God, tell these stones to become loaves of bread" (Matthew 4:3, NLT).

But Jesus was ready. He knew his father, and he knew the scriptures. He quoted Deuteronomy 8:3: "But Jesus told him, 'No! The Scriptures say, People do not live by bread alone, but by every word that comes from the mouth of God.'" (Matthew 4:4, NLT)

We live off what we consume.

My spiritual health is much like my physical health. If I am filling my belly with junk, I won't be healthy in the long run even if it tastes delicious and I feel full in that moment.

Similarly, if the things I do with my time and what I read and see are junk, they might feel good in the moment but my spirituality will be unhealthy in the long run.

The long run is going to come up sooner than you think.

If having a baby means you feel justified to turn your attention away from Jesus because it's just not a good time, having a toddler won't make it feel easier.

And having your kids finally off to school won't make it feel easier either.

I haven't lived my whole life yet, but I assume the same excuses will accompany me as long as I let them.

We cannot wait until the kids move out and we retire to sit down to focus on Jesus. If we do that, then we've missed out on having Jesus accompany us on this amazing journey of life. We've missed Jesus accompanying us through our parenting journey. We've missed having Jesus walk us through our marriage. Jesus will have missed every high, every low, and all the mundane things that he wants to be with us for. He will not have been our companion through any of it. I don't know about you, but I want to walk my whole life with Jesus. I don't want to catch him up on things at the end.

When do we need to prioritize Jesus?

The time is now. The time is now to start that journey. Right where you are. Exactly how busy you are is the right amount of busy. Jesus knows. He knows how much you have to meet him with. He wants you to come anyway.

His offer is wholesome, nutritious, and it will leave you feeling satisfied. And in the long run, you will feel the health accumulate from your choices.

You were not meant to live on bread alone. You were also created to live on the Word of God.

Declaration

For you have been born again, not of perishable seed, but of imperishable, through the living and enduring word of God (1 Peter 1:23, NIV).

Questions

What types of "spiritual junk food" do you find satisfying but know is not really that healthy?

What are the lies you tell yourself to justify feeding yourself and your life with things that will not leave you healthy in the long run?

Prayer

Write a prayer asking God to show you an area of your life where you feel satisfied but are really settling for an empty substitute. Ask him to show you how he can satisfy you in a real way instead.

Day 34:
Fixing our Eyes

In the first few weeks of the COVID 19 pandemic and while on a family hike to escape being stuck inside, God whispered Isaiah 43:18-19 to my heart: "Forget the former things; do not dwell on the past. See, I am doing a new thing! Now it springs up; do you not perceive it? I am making a way in the wilderness and streams in the wasteland" (NIV).

The seasons were changing. COVID 19 had changed everything. It wasn't shocking this verse was brought up to my heart.

In fact, anyone could see that there were unthinkable changes everywhere. God didn't need to tell me something that I already knew. He wanted to bring my attention to the unseen. God had so much more in mind than I could even know.

As it turned out, that verse wasn't just about making my way through a pandemic.

I now realize looking back that God was trying to prepare my heart for a bigger transition. In that same week, I feel like God had shouted at me, "I want you to go back to your old church." Since church was only online at that point, it was not a very big stretch for me to log in to the service at a church we had left two and a half years before the pandemic started.

But as the practicality of returning to our old church in person became a real step that we would need to take in the physical, I wasn't sure that I was willing to thrust my children into such a dramatic change.

2 Corinthians 4:17-18 says, "For our light and momentary troubles are achieving for us an eternal glory that far outweighs them all. So we fix our eyes not on what is seen, but on what is unseen, since what is seen is temporary, but what is unseen is eternal" (NIV).

While I wrestled this out in prayer with God, I felt him remind me over and over again that I cannot look to what I see as truth. I cannot look to what I see as what I will need to make this decision. If I add things together in an earthly way, I will get an earthly sum. But he wanted me to trust that his math multiplies instead of adds.

When I worried that my kids would not adjust to a new church, He just kept saying, "trust me." Isaiah 43 kept seeping back into my mind. He is doing a new thing. Some days I just didn't see it.

When my kids did have a difficult day at church and felt lonely, God kept telling me to look at him and not at the momentary struggle in front of me.

Staying in God's Word day after day is where I found my faith to trust in what I cannot see.

"The unfolding of your words gives light; it gives understanding to the simple" (Psalm 119:130, NIV).

I may not always see things in the physical, but God's Word brings clarity to the eternal. Even if I see things in my heart before I see them in the physical, the Word of God will bring clarity to my earthly blindness. My eyes can only see the physical. They do not see eternity. But his eyes do. And his Word endures for all time. When we read the Word of God, we are opening up our vision into eternity. It opens our spiritual eyes to see more.

We need this type of vision if we are to navigate through this world. We need this type of vision to lead us through the wilderness. Things are not as they always appear.

If you've ever needed glasses, you know the difference in your vision between having them on or off. Sometimes when I am driving, I need to switch my regular glasses for sunglasses if the sun comes out or vice versa. There is a moment between glasses where I am not wearing either. My vision is very blurry. It looks like the road I was driving on moments before, but I really cannot see it clearly.

Our time with Jesus is like wearing the correct prescription glasses to walk through life. When we forgo our time with God for other things, it can start to feel like we are wandering through the wilderness without the right prescription and everything may seem blurry or unclear. We do not have eternal clarity. Just like we may need glasses to see clearly in a physical way we need a spiritual prescription to fill the gap between our earthly understanding and his eternal view.

Jesus can fill the gap between temporary and eternal. His voice becomes our vision and He will lead us through the wasteland. There is so much to life we cannot see without a "God prescription".

And returning to Isaiah 43:18-19: a few years after God whispered that verse to my heart, I can answer him. Yes, I did perceive you doing a new thing. I could see it with my godly perspective even when I couldn't see it with my earthly prospective.

God has done remarkable things in that transition. We feel at home at our new church now.

Fitted with the right prescription that allows us to see his eternal vision, the direction of our lives will be clear. Through his Word, we see there is a path forged through the wilderness with love.

Declaration

I remain confident of this: I will see the goodness of the Lord in the land of the living (Psalm 27:13, NIV).

Questions

Have you perceived God shifting things in a direction you didn't understand? Did you seek understanding or did you fight what He was doing? What was the outcome of trusting or fighting what God was doing?

Did you ever have the wrong perspective on something where your earthly understanding was lacking? When did you figure out that God knew what you did not have eyes to see?

Is there an area of your life that you would like more understanding and Godly wisdom?

Prayer

Write a prayer to Jesus asking him to give you a clearer understanding of something he is doing that you do not yet understand. Ask him to fill the gap between what you can see and what he can see with his eternal perspective.

Day 35:
The Shadows

After starting my journey into daily Bible reading and praying, I did actually start seeing the fruits of being connected to God. However, the day-to-day reading didn't always feel like crazy shifts were happening in my heart and my life. It sometimes felt mundane. And frequently I would encounter situations where all the work that God was doing on the inside and all of the scripture I was taking in was having a hard time staying in.

"A good man brings good things out of the good stored up in his heart, and an evil man brings evil things out of the evil stored up in his heart. For the mouth speaks what the heart is full of" (Luke 6:45, NIV).

I've heard it said that behind anger is usually pain. Well then, the opposite must be true! Behind a sense of calm, there is a lot of joy and contentment. Think about how you feel when you are soaking in the Word of God and feel connected to his presence. Bible reading and time with Jesus produces an abundance of peace, comfort, and patience.

There were times when I would speak up in Bible studies with truth and love and I would leave afterwards feeling like, "Was that really just me who said all that?" I didn't grow up in a Christian home. Those weren't truths I memorized in Sunday School. I was speaking out of a close relationship with and growth in the knowledge of Jesus Christ. On one particular occasion, I left a women's group wondering if it was me speaking or if the Holy Spirit had taken over my tongue. When you fill your soul with nourishing truth, you cannot hold it in. We were not made to take the Word of God in without putting the Word of God out into the world.

"Neither do people light a lamp and put it under a bowl. Instead, they put it on its stand, and it gives light to everyone in the house" (Matthew 5:15, NIV).

Jesus has done so many incredible things in my life. I cannot help but talk and tell of the remarkable things he has done. And you won't be able to stop yourself from the light of God's Word shining out of you either.

There is one thing I realized though. As this light began to shine from me, I noticed something a bit frightening.

Shadows.

For a shadow to exist, there needs to be a light source.

Sometimes when you rise up as a light for Christ and when Christ's light shines out of you, you will see dark shadows appear. Your light will cause a shadow to be cast where your light doesn't break through.

You are not responsible for your light to illuminate everything. Many people did not recognize or appreciate Jesus, who was himself the light of the world.

"The true light that gives light to everyone was coming into the world. He was in the world, and though the world was made through him, the world did not recognize him. He came to that which was his own, but his own did not receive him" (John 1:10-11, NIV).

Rise up anyway. Jesus didn't slow down when others did not see what he was doing.

People may not like that you spend time in your Bible. People may not like the changes that Jesus makes in your heart. Sometimes you may even scare yourself a little when you feel God shifting your heart in ways that you didn't expect or when he releases you from things you wanted to hold tightly to. The opposition you face will cast a shadow. But it is a sign to you that you are shining when you see those shadows. You are not doing anything wrong.

Do not let these shadows scare you! You are illuminated from the inside out by a light source that is far greater than any worldly spotlight. As a light that can only work when plugged into an outlet, you will shine God's love when you are plugged into the Word of God.

Declaration

In the same way, let your light shine before others, that they may see your good deeds and glorify your Father in heaven (Matthew 5:16, NIV).

Questions

Is there a time when you had to stand up and speak God's truth? How did it feel? Did you feel equipped?

Was there ever a time and place you sat quietly and wished you had the courage to speak God's truth into the world? What do you think held you back?

Have you had negative or positive reactions to sharing God's truth? Why do you think the reactions were positive or negative? How did it feel?

Prayer

Write a prayer of gratefulness and gratitude towards Jesus for the ways that he has filled areas of your life with his light. Try to remember the ways that he has brought light into darkness. Invite him in to light up areas of darkness that you still have.

Day 36:
The Narrow Gate

"You can enter God's Kingdom only through the narrow gate. The highway to hell is broad, and its gate is wide for the many who choose that way. But the gateway to life is very narrow and the road is difficult, and only a few ever find it" (Matthew 7:13-14, NLT).

I heard a story once about a high school graduating class that chose the AC/DC song Highway to Hell as their graduation song.

I want to believe this is an urban legend, because it's so horrifying! And while there is a chance this was never actually true, I think there would be a lot of grade 12 students who would find the idea hilarious.

I am willing to bet that if you've picked up this book, you are hopeful that you have found the narrow gate and avoided the highway to hell. But I sometimes wonder: if it is so hard to find, then how can I know that I have found it? This isn't like checking the blue dot on my phone when I am following directions on Google Maps.

I can't even find the raspberry jam in my fridge when my kids are having breakfast! How can I find the gateway to life? Sounds like it's hidden behind more than just a pickle jar.

I want to take you to Mark 6:45 to look deeper into this search. Let me set the stage for you. Jesus and his disciples had just fed 5000 families. The Bible tells us, "Immediately after this, Jesus insisted that his disciples get back into the boat and head across the lake to Bethsaida, while he sent the people home" (NLT)

> Late that night, the disciples were in their boat in the middle of the lake, and Jesus was alone on land. He saw that they were in serious trouble, rowing hard and struggling against the wind and waves. About three o'clock in the morning, Jesus came

> toward them, walking on the water. He intended to go past them, but when they saw him walking on the water, they cried out in terror, thinking he was a ghost. They were all terrified when they saw him. But Jesus spoke to them at once. "Don't be afraid," he said. "Take courage! I am here!" Then he climbed into the boat, and the wind stopped. They were totally amazed (Mark 6:47-51, NLT).

Jesus gave his disciples clear directions to go across the lake to Bethsaida that night. Yet they still encountered a storm big enough to scare them. The Bible tells us they were struggling against the winds. If they had turned the boat around when they came up to the storm and headed back in the opposite direction and ignored Jesus' directions, they would have found rowing easier. The wind would have been at their backs. But they would have been headed in the wrong direction. Jesus told them to cross the lake, even though he knew it meant they would still encounter a storm. He knew the right way to go wouldn't be smooth sailing.

However, Jesus met them in the middle of that storm. He climbed into the boat. He told them not to be afraid and to have courage. Jesus being present with them is what calmed the storm, not running away from it.

The road to the narrow gate does not promise the absence of storms. But it does promise the presence of God.

Don't we often feel like the easiest path must be from God? If something feels easy, then that must be the direction he wants us to head. Sometimes God does close doors, but he doesn't remove troubles or hard times. Matthew 7:14 states, "the road is difficult, and only a few ever find it" (NLT). But as the lyrics to the song Highway to Hell say: "Livin' easy".

Spending time with God daily isn't going to be easy. That is why the people around you aren't doing it regularly. But that isn't an excuse.

In James 1:2-4 we are instructed to, "Count it all joy, my brothers, when you meet trials of various kinds, for you know that the testing of your faith produces steadfastness. And let steadfastness have its full effect, that you may be perfect and complete, lacking in nothing" (ESV).

The road to the narrow gate does not promise we won't have plenty of trials. James is saying that it is through these trials we will know we are on the right path. Just as the disciples discovered in the boat that night: the storm actually brought Jesus closer to them.

Do any of the statements below fit your life?

My spiritual life is without battles.

God isn't asking me to do difficult or impossible things that require a leap of faith.

Everyone around me is doing the same things that I am.

My spiritual life feels comfortable and safe.

My spiritual life involves showing up only requiring to be "fed".

I choose what is easiest most often, believing God will show me the way through all obstacles.

If any of these statements feel accurate, take heart. The narrow path is hard to find, but not impossible.

Sometimes we get off track. We wander off the path and back into the crowd. We know we want the narrow road. It can get scary. It can get lonely. It can be hard. But keep getting back on track. Keep opening your Bible and pointing yourself toward Jesus in every way you can. He will get in the boat with you and make sure you make it through the storm and to your destination.

Declaration

That is why, for Christ's sake, I delight in weakness, in insults, in hardships, in persecutions, in difficulties. For when I am weak, then I am strong (2 Corinthians 12:10, NIV).

Questions

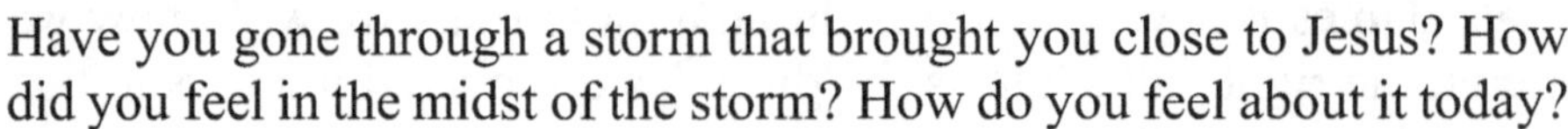

Have you gone through a storm that brought you close to Jesus? How did you feel in the midst of the storm? How do you feel about it today?

When one of the storms of life hit, what is your first reaction? Do you run towards it or away from it?

From the list of statements in this devotional that may or may not describe your spiritual life, which if any describe your spiritual life most accurately? How have you justified living your spiritual life this way?

Prayer

Write a prayer asking God to show you the path to the narrow gate. If you see the path but you find it hard to stay on course, ask God to create a desire in your heart to stay headed in the right direction and a desire to walk this narrow path. Confess what is pulling you off course.

Day 37:
Wisdom is Calling

I scanned the mail my mom had dropped off in my bedroom. A few weeks earlier, I had applied to attend a Bible School in Sweden. I was about to finish my final semester of university and I was considering going there for a semester after graduation. To my shock, there was already an envelope from the school in my hand. It was my acceptance letter! But I was not ready to make a decision. I applied to keep my options open, not because I wanted to make a quick decision. I had some very real pros and cons in mind. But I needed more. I needed wisdom.

Facts are not enough. We've never had more access to information in all of history! But that does not mean that we are making the wisest decisions in human history either.

I prayed and asked God what he wanted me to do. The answer became apparent to me. However, I still decided not to make a solid commitment immediately. I had the wisdom right in front of me. My heart knew what I should do, and I felt peaceful about it. But I still hesitated to fully commit to that choice. Something in me kept doubting and ignoring wisdom. I was afraid to close doors. Having options can feel safer than making commitments.

We often want to make decisions on our own and feel that we are smart enough to do so. We ignore or often choose to disregard the wisdom God pours out generously (as I did in this case).

James 1:5-8 says:

> If any of you lacks wisdom, you should ask God, who gives generously to all without finding fault, and it will be given to you. But when you ask, you must believe and not doubt, because the one who doubts is like a wave of the sea, blown and tossed by the wind. That person should not expect to receive anything from the Lord. Such a person is double-

> minded and unstable in all they do (NIV).

So why did I hesitate so much? In retrospect, I was being double-minded and unstable. I spent more time in that place that I should have. I doubted. I let the feelings I had day-to-day start to impact my momentum towards the direction I felt called to go.

We need to ask for the wisdom God provides us. And then we need to accept it.

These beautiful verses are a reminder to me why I shouldn't hesitate. I will never be able to predict or manipulate anything into something beautiful the way God can.

> Joyful is the person who finds wisdom, the one who gains understanding. For wisdom is more profitable than silver and her wages are better than gold. Wisdom is more precious than rubies; nothing you desire can compare with her. She offers you long life in her right hand, and riches and honor in her left. She will guide you down delightful paths; all her ways are satisfying. Wisdom is a tree of life to those who embrace her; happy are those who hold her tightly (Proverbs 3:13-18, NIV).

We need to come to God for wisdom and guidance. We need to set our time aside to enjoy the wisdom of God, because there is so much abundance there. I feel tossed around like I am out at sea without an anchor when I am functioning without the wisdom of God.

Are you satisfied with how doing things your way using your own understanding is working out? Or will you open your heart to wisdom and accept that God may be leading you towards something better that you do not yet understand?

"Trust in the Lord with all your heart and lean not on your own understanding; in all your ways submit to him, and he will make your paths straight" (Proverbs 3:5-6, NIV).

There is a way that is not YOUR way that leads to abundant life. Will you surrender to what God wants to do? Ask him! And go after the pathways he shows you.

We too often live on the opinions of others, the direction of popular culture, and the overabundance of information flooding our minds. Sometimes I do not know what I want. So, I need to go back and refocus on what God wants.

Back to my own decision. It didn't look like a sane choice to go to Bible School, from the outside. I had to trust God to provide in so many ways. I had to leave my life behind for a time. I had to put off starting a career and continuing on with my life. To my non-Christian parents, this was utter foolishness. But because I listened to the wisdom of God, I began a journey where I found delightful paths. Paths that have led to you reading these words today because of that decision back then.

God doesn't leave us like a ship at sea being tossed and turned. He offers us wisdom and stability in the storms.

He will give you his wisdom if you ask. But you will need to step out in faith and follow the delightful paths that Wisdom is calling you to.

Declaration

I will instruct you and teach you in the way you should go; I will counsel you with my loving eye on you (Psalm 32:8, NIV).

Questions

In what area of your life do you need wisdom? Do you have any decisions that you need to make right now? What are they?

Prayer

Write out a prayer asking God for wisdom in this area. When you are finished, take 30 seconds in silence and listen to what the Holy Spirit wants to say. Then write it down. Take a few quiet moments throughout the day to repeat this prayer.

Day 38:
Holding on to Your Treasure

Taking possession of the house we built was a huge milestone for my husband and I. The moment came when we got the key from the builder, and of course we had to snap a picture of that "key in the door" moment. It was the accumulation of our life savings and nine months of time and energy picking everything out and watching it come together.

Now that it is ours, we have a key. There is a lock on the door because it needs protecting. We don't want anyone to just wander in and live here or have access to our stuff. I also wouldn't go and throw my key to anyone on the street who asked for it. Who knows what they would do with it!

There will be people, situations, or seasons that may tempt us to throw away all the valuable treasure we have stored up during our walk with Jesus.

If we wouldn't throw away the key to our earthly belongings, why do we throw away our valuable spiritual treasures?

What does this look like? We might fill our schedules with extra commitments that seem to promise us so much but cost us that time with Jesus.

We let snarky comments or unhealed pain affect our emotions.

There may be observations or remarks from people who do not like the outward changes in us that come from the inward work we are doing. Not everyone is going to be happy with your spiritual growth.

We can be our own worst enemies and self destruct on things like scrolling social media or numbing with food or TV instead of deepening our relationship with Jesus.

In the Sermon on the Mount Jesus gives this warning:

"Do not give dogs what is sacred; do not throw your pearls to pigs. If you do, they may trample them under their feet, and turn and tear you to pieces" (Matthew 7:6, NIV).

We need to protect the treasure we have built in our hearts, whether it be from our own sinful ways or from other people and influences.

It is an all-out war for our souls.

The more treasure you accumulate in your walk with God, the more the enemy will be out to steal it and the more others may try to trample your pearls.

I want you to see the value in what you are accumulating as you go deeper and build long-lasting, solid routines and a relationship with Jesus. There is a sacredness in your heart that you need to protect. There is so much that God is going to do and there is so much that God has already done. The enemy wants you to forget that and throw it to the pigs. Do not turn around and surrender all that time and energy to what is unholy. Because one day, it will turn around and attack you.

But make no mistake. What you are accomplishing is precious. It will need protecting, just like the home we built needed protecting with a lock and key. My prayer is that you grow so close to Jesus that you will protect your relationship carefully and never want to throw it away.

Declaration

Above all else, guard your heart, for everything you do flows from it (Proverbs 4:23, NIV).

Questions

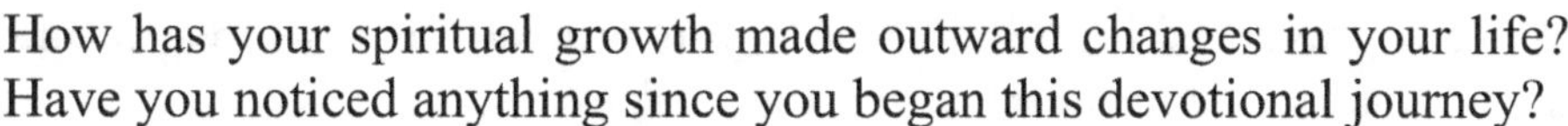

How has your spiritual growth made outward changes in your life? Have you noticed anything since you began this devotional journey?

In what ways do you find yourself sabotaging your own spiritual growth?

Have you ever shared with someone about your spiritual growth? Can you think of a time it was well received? Was there a time it was not well received?

Prayer

Write a prayer asking God to help you protect the treasures he has accumulated in your heart along this journey.

Day 39:
Subtracting a Negative

My official degree is a Bachelor of Education. I used to be a math teacher. While it's been a while since I was in the classroom, I still remember a lot of basic math. I hope you had great math teachers so you will remember just a little bit for this devotional!

I also hope that by this point in our journey together you realize that you definitely need to spend more time with God and that this is one of the best things you can do with your life. But perhaps you're still thinking that you just cannot find ways to make it work. It is still hard. I completely understand. The list of distractions and responsibilities are endless. We are expected to be everything and do everything. We are also supposed to do it with a smile. But that is simply not achievable, and it isn't life giving.

What if instead of just adding good things to our lives, we first start by taking away the things that are not giving life to our souls?

My guess is that you have a lot of idle time that you aren't really using for good. It could be the mindless scrolling of TikTok videos or the Netflix you watch. It could be video games, or romance novels, Instagram, or YouTube. What are the things that take time away from God in YOUR life? It's time to admit that there are things that you do that are not adding good into your life. There are things you spend your time on that are not life-giving. There are things you know you should spend less time doing, but you don't and it's hard. I get it.

I want you to write those things down now: *(see next page for additional space)*

Now, I want you to go back and circle the ones you are honestly willing to give up to make more space for Jesus. It's okay if you are not willing to give up everything, or even give something up entirely. We are just trying to make a bit of space.

Back to my math lesson.

Somewhere in junior high you probably started to learn how to add, subtract, multiply, and divide with negative numbers.

Remember that when you subtract a negative, you are actually adding a positive:

$5 - (-2) = 5 + 2 = 7$

I could go into a deeper explanation of why, but if you don't believe me, you can grab your calculator and verify my answer.

If you have to add a positive to subtract a negative in math, could it work the same for your spiritual life? Do you need to add good to cancel out the bad?

If you take away a negative in your life, you will actually have to add a positive for the math to work.

We need to create beautiful habits and rhythms to put in our life if we are going to keep moving forward. Those negatives will seem all too enticing without added positives to replace them.

What positives are you going to add in order to take those negatives away?

Please take a moment and read through the appendix on page 193 to get some ideas for spending more time with Jesus. I want you to take a moment and write down the ones that you can start doing today. The ones you know you can fit into your lifestyle, that jive with your skills, personality, strengths, etc. I know this isn't going to be easy, but it will bring good things such as growth, peace, and life. There will be times when you get busy and wrapped up in life activities. I have written this entire devotional to try to empower you with the truth that you need to have time with God daily in your life. You've been doing life far too long without Jesus deeply engrained in your day. You haven't been holding his hand as much as you want to.

Since this is our second last devotional together, I am going to switch things up a little bit. So now, instead of me writing to you about why you need to do this, I want you to take a moment and write a letter to yourself about why you are doing this. What do you want to tell yourself when you feel like giving up? What encouragement are you going to need? When you are done, tuck the page in your Bible. You can even use it as your bookmark. Space for this can be found on the next page.

Let me pray with you first.

Heavenly Father, I thank you for the person reading this book right now. I pray that you would guide them into the smallest steps of getting started. That they will write to themselves exactly what they are going to need to remind themselves when life gets busy and time with you becomes difficult. Let them write the words they will need to hear when those moments come.

Dear _________,

Day 40:
He Who Began a Good Work in You

As we come to the end of our time together, there is something that I want to share with you that I haven't told you yet. Now that you have gotten to know a bit about me and my walk with Jesus through my adult life, I think now is the time that I want to share with you a bit about me before I grew up and started walking out this faith journey.

I wasn't raised in a Christian home. Aside from a few friends bringing me to church, there were a handful of times my parents took my brother and I to church simply to show us what it was. But there were no kids at this church. There was no Sunday School. Nobody ever explained to me what all of this was. I had to sit still in a pew in an uncomfortable dress and pay attention to something that I didn't understand. Then I had to wait in the lobby until whenever my parents decided to leave. Running around through overly-perfumed ladies and men shaking out their hankies to blow their noses was not fun for me. I preferred Sundays where I got to enjoy sleeping in and lounging around the house. It was chaos and fighting to get out the door when we did go to church. So, I didn't like church. It's a good thing it only happened a few times. Years of that would have worn me down hard.

Then at 16, a friend brought me to her youth group. Although there were seeds planted by friends when I was growing up, this was the very first time I set foot in a youth group worship service. I decided to give my life to Jesus. Some would stay I started late. It felt like I was always so many steps behind everyone else.

It took three years before I found my own church. In university I went to Campus for Christ meetings. But I would sit in the back and hope they wouldn't make me participate.

You see, from these humble beginnings I have somehow managed to string an entire devotional book together. I think the girl who originally brought me to church looked at my feeble efforts to try to fit in with a church group and felt pity for me. It was clear I didn't know anything and I didn't belong.

Yet here I am.

By the power of the Holy Spirit, here I am. All the glory to God. This is not because of my own effort. Yes, I initiated, but Jesus really did the rest. I opened my Bible, I signed up for the group, I said the prayer. But Jesus did the life change in me. I am still a work in progress. We all are. But it had to begin somewhere. As I came near to God, he came near to me.

I've come from being an outsider sitting on the floor of the balcony in a church youth group not knowing where to start to a woman in a relationship with Jesus that has changed everything. You are holding in your hands right now proof of the possibilities in your own life.

Paul wrote these words to the church in Philippi, but I believe these words are just as true for you and me today:

"In all my prayers for all of you, I always pray with joy because of your partnership in the gospel from the first day until now, being confident of this, that he who began a good work in you will carry it on to completion until the day of Christ Jesus" (Philippians 1:3-6, NIV).

Jesus has so much more in store for all of us. I have thought of you over and over and prayed for you as I have written all these words. Know that Christ has begun a work in me and he wants to do the same in you. Though it may not seem like it every day, I promise you that he is doing a good work in you and he will continue to do so.

There were so many days I sat at my computer and I didn't feel like I made any progress on my book. There were days I felt like I didn't know if I could ever write enough that even made sense. But day after day, and after over a year of little tiny increments of work and progress on my book, I am sitting here typing the last devotional to you with a stack of 39 others beside me. One word at a time. One day at a time. I am sincerely overwhelmed at what God did with the tiny bits I gave him day after day.

What you are holding in your hand is a reminder that the smallest planted seeds will grow. One step at a time, an athlete finishes a marathon. One step with Jesus at a time equals a life walked out with him by our side. We do not need to wait any longer to begin to allow Jesus to carry out this good work in us.

The time is now.

Declaration

And the one sitting on the throne said, "Look, I am making everything new!" And then he said to me, "Write this down, for what I tell you is trustworthy and true" (Revelation 21:5, NLT).

Questions

In the last 40 days, what has impacted you the most? Take a moment and write down some of the most important things that you have read. Perhaps you need to take a moment and flip back through these pages and see what stood out most. Write those points down here:

Prayer

Write a prayer asking God to help you protect the truths he has revealed to your heart during this journey and to show you what he has planned for the next part of your journey together.

Appendix
How to Connect with Jesus

I've gathered some ideas here for connecting with Jesus. Before you read through the list, I just want to say one quick thing.

The God of the universe gave us the Bible. However, there are many books, podcasts, and sermons you can listen to. You can sit in church week after week and hear the sermons and sing the songs. But you still may not feel like your soul is satisfied.

There is not going to be anything better than reading his Word straight from the source. So, while I encourage you to engage with other ways to interact with Jesus, I would say there is still no substitute for simply reading the Bible and praying. It sounds so simple, doesn't it? But all through history we have never had more access to Jesus-based media. We can scroll social media accounts dedicated to Jesus. We can download podcasts and listen to them anywhere. But let's not forget that even with many other ways to access Jesus-based media, the Bible is THE Word of God.

There is so much noise in this world, and if we do not take steps to tune out the noise it will be so much harder to hear God. We first need to turn down the noise of the world before turning up Jesus.

If my husband decides to listen to loud music in my living room but I would like to sit and listen to a podcast, I do not turn up my podcast and try to drown out the sound of his music. I ask him to turn it off, or give him headphones, or I put in my headphones. We don't silence noise with noise. We first turn down what we need to hear less of, then we turn up the volume on what we want to hear.

Here are some ideas for turning up Jesus in your life:

- Open up your Bible and just begin. It can literally be that simple. Start at the beginning or just pick a book. In my opinion, the Gospel of John is a great book to start with.

- Set a timer and sit in silence for one minute. Listen to God. You can increase the length of time as you choose. But start with one minute.

- Start a Bible reading plan. You can find many online. If you have a Bible app there will be reading plans available there too.

- Download podcasts to listen to while you are doing laundry, walking, exercising, or doing dishes. Buy a pair of wireless headphones to make this even easier.

- YouTube has many sermons to listen to. Sometimes I find it helpful to watch, not just listen. I watch these sermons on my treadmill or while I am eating lunch.

- Find a devotional book to start reading after you finish this one.

- Write down your prayers, both short term and long term. Visit them daily and pray for them. When you have a list in front of you it is much easier to focus on it, and writing down the answers to those prayers or the ways that God has re-directed you to a different outcome is exciting!

- Subscribe to a daily devotional email list.

- When you wake up in the morning, put your phone aside until you have spent five minutes reading the Bible.

- Ask a friend to join you, and check in daily to keep each other accountable.

- Go outside in nature and connect with God there.

- Memorize scripture verses that you feel deep connection with so they can be helpful weapons of spiritual warfare.

- Find ways to serve God. This could mean stepping up and volunteering at church or finding ways to serve in your community.

- Start a gratitude journal and give thanks to God for what he has provided and all the ways he has worked in your life and IS working in your life. You can then take this list out and pray thanks over it again and again and add to it regularly.

- Share prayer requests with a friend and check in weekly.

- Find a verse and meditate on it for a week. Be ready to journal ways God brings that verse to life!

- Read scripture out loud. The enemy cannot know your thoughts. Much like reading daily declarations, this is a way to speak truth over the enemy because he has no power over words of truth.

- If you play a musical instrument, learn a worship song and sing along!

- Download an audiobook of the Bible or stream it off a Bible app.

- Write a song or poem.

- Fast. This does not have be just about food! Give up something you will miss and replace that time and focus with Jesus.

- Paint or draw something that you feel spiritually moved to create.

- Tithe. If you already give 10%, try and give a bit more. Are there organizations or charities that are close to your heart? That might be a place to start going above and beyond.

- Create a prayer room or area in your home.

- Start family devotional time. Find suitable devotions to do with your kids that are age appropriate.

- Start a devotional time with your spouse. This can be as simple as reading through the Bible together.

- Choose more Christian movies to watch instead of secular ones.

- Journal. There are many types of Christian journals available with prompts to get you started.

Add your own ideas here:

As you can see, there is not just one way to do this. There is no minimum time requirement. But when I read these ideas, I get excited! There are so many easy and practical ways to engage with Jesus on a daily basis. Every single one of us has a heart created by Jesus, for Jesus. Ask him to lead you to what will work and I promise you that you will find something that truly makes you come alive and feel connected with him.

References

Government of Canada. (2019, September 12). *Radiation health effects*. Canadian Nuclear Safety Commission. https://www.cnsc-ccsn.gc.ca/eng/resources/radiation/radiation-health-effects/

Chodosh, S. (2018, September 22). *When a plane loses pressure, here's what happens to your body*. https://Https://www.popsci.com/what-happens-to-your-body-when-plane-loses-pressure

English Standard Version Bible. (2001). Crossway. https://www.biblegateway.com/versions/english-standard-version-esv-bible/

Jenkins, P. (2021, June 15). *Target fixation: Staying focused.* Live on Purpose. https://drpauljenkins.com/target-fixation-staying-focused/

Naoumidis, A. (2020, June 25). *Highway hypnosis: What is it and what does it tell us about ourselves?* Mindset Health. https://www.mindsethealth.com/matter/highway-hypnosis

New International Version Bible. (2011). Biblica. https://www.biblegateway.com/versions/new-international-version-niv-bible/

New Living Translation Bible. (1996). Tyndale. New Living Translation (NLT) - Version Information - BibleGateway.com

Merriam-Webster. (n.d.). *Sowing*. https://www.merriam-webster.com/dictionary/sowing

The Message Bible. (2018). NavPress. https://www.biblegateway.com/versions/Message-MSG-Bible

Rutledge, K., McDaniel, M., Teng, S., Hall, H., Ramroop, T., Sprout, E., Hunt, J., Boudreau, D., & Costa, H. (2023, October 19). *Understanding rivers*. National Geographic. https://education.nationalgeographic.org/resource/understanding-rivers/

Trueman, S. (2020, November 20). *Phototropism explained.* ThoughtCo. https://www.thoughtco.com/phototropism-419215

Witze, A. (2019). *A deeper understanding of the Grand Canyon.* Knowable Magazine. https://doi.org/10.1146/knowable-022619-1

World Health Organization. (2023, July 27). *Ionizing radiation and health effects*. Fact Sheets. https://www.who.int/news-room/fact-sheets/detail/ionizing-radiation-and-health-effects

About the Author

Katie Bergen is a wife and a mom to two children. She lives in Edmonton, Alberta, Canada. She is passionate about inspiring women to find the abundant life Jesus promised and to encourage them to live confidently as daughters of Christ. When she is not writing, she loves spending her time hiking in the mountains, paddleboarding, and running.

www.ingramcontent.com/pod-product-compliance
Lightning Source LLC
LaVergne TN
LVHW012052160826
845678LV00014B/2791

* 9 7 8 1 0 6 8 9 0 7 7 0 8 *